One Way To Write SHORT STORIES

Ben Nyberg

Cincinnati, Ohio

For MLN

"The Reasonable Request," by Sally V. Doud, © 1981 by *Kansas Quarterly*, is reprinted by permission of Sally Doud.

"Turmoil," by Anton Chekhov, translated from Russian by Franklin D. Reeve is reprinted by permission of F. D. Reeve.

"A Matter of Conscience," by Ona Angela Wooley, is reprinted by permission of Ona Angela Wooley.

"Cracks in the Sidewalk," by Linda Funk, is reprinted by permission of Linda L. Funk.

 Published by Writer's Digest Books, an imprint of F&W Publications, Inc., 1507 Dana Ave., Cincinnati, Ohio 45207. First edition.

---

92 91 90 89 88   5 4 3 2 1

Library of Congress Cataloging-in-Publication Data

Nyberg, Ben, 1933-
One great way to write short stories.
Includes index.
1. Short story—Authorship. I. Title.
PN3373.N94 1988   808.3'1   88-10770
ISBN 0-89879-327-0

**Primer: a beginner's book of basic principles.*
**Primer: something that primes.*

ACKNOWLEDGMENTS

A book is a gift, and a debt. As for the gift, I only hope it may reach those whose need it was written to serve. Regarding the debt, I'm obliged to too many colleagues, friends, editors, and former students to try mentioning them all individually. But some few I must thank by name for their part in making the book happen. Thanks to Earle Davis, Fred Higginson, Richard McGhee, and Harry Donaghy, Kansas State University English Department Heads during the period 1965-1987, for fostering a work environment that enabled this project to ripen over time. To Robert Rechnitz, for getting the ball rolling. To G. W. Clift, Robin Mosher, James Wilson, Roger Friedmann, and Grant Tracey, for testing the method in practice and helping clarify its procedures and presentation. To Marion Dane Bauer, for reading the manuscript in its final stages and suggesting a number of useful improvements. To Frank Reeve for generously preparing his fine new translation of Chekhov's "Turmoil" especially for this book. To Sally Doud for the use of her original story, "The Reasonable Request," reprinted from *Kansas Quarterly.* To Linda Funk and Angie Wooley for the use of their "Primer Method" stories. (I must note that although no final draft version of Linda's story appears at the end of Chapter Nine, she did finish and type it up—a submission-ready manuscript titled "Cracks in the Sidewalk.") To Nan Dibble and Jean Fredette, whose sound editorial sense and commitment to excellence made refining final copy both challenging and rewarding. Lastly, to my wife Lyndal, for always being ready to read every page, often many times over, till the words at last seemed right, and for patience, tact, support and good cheer.

CONTENTS

TO ALL WHO WOULD WRITE A STORY IF THEY ONLY KNEW HOW

As its title says, this book describes an approach to writing stories. It is an approach I have developed over more than twenty years of helping people learn how to write fiction. About ten years ago I set down the essentials of this technique in a series of "lessons" which I christened *The Fiction Primer*. A reworked version of that manuscript, *The Short Story Primer*, was eventually accepted for publication by Writer's Digest Books. It is the book you now hold in your hands.

The "great way" to write a story that this book teaches is what I call "Primer Method." It's a strategy for crafting short fiction that pledges to pull an honest-to-goodness story from anyone ready to follow its rules. Which is why it really is both a *primer*—a beginner's book of basic principles—and a *primer*—a device that primes and gets things flowing. Stay with it, step by step, and you'll have an original short story to show for it: that's the promise that sets *The Primer* method apart from other systems or techniques of fiction writing.

Most books on story writing are more "descriptive" than "directive." They speak in general terms about the creative process and those qualities of good fiction that every aspiring writer ought to strive for. Such books are often written by successful practicing writers, and so are ordinarily a pleasure to read. At their best they offer a collection of personal insights "straight from the horse's mouth" that can boost the morale and beef up the commitment of apprentice writers by offering them a star to steer by and a creed to follow.

But even at their best these books don't give beginners much practical help with the nuts-and-bolts work of actually building a short story. Most contain useful technical tips and some even try to lay out a rough work plan. What they don't get around to is spelling out specific procedures, giving step-by-step directions for going from start to finish of the whole building process.

There are several reasons for this. First of all, fiction gets written so many different ways, it's hard to say anything specific on that subject which will *always* hold true. So it's safer to stick to generalizations. Second, the nature and sources of fictional "matter" and how to shape it into finished works of art are hard topics to get into without either oversimplifying the concepts involved or overwhelming the reader with lots of abstract terms. So it's simpler to sidestep these thorny problems than to try coping with them. Finally, storywriters themselves are sometimes guilty of deliberately pulling the wool over innocent eyes by pretending that the whole creative process is some kind of mystical secret that gets revealed to the elect but can never be learned by ordinary mortals. Certainly no formulaic method could ever be used to craft respectable stories. Since low-grade "pulp" fiction is written to a formula, the circular logic goes, it must mean that to use a formula is to produce pulp.

The Primer is guided by the belief that it can't hurt the cause of fiction to explain as clearly as possible how it works and how ordinary literate persons can construct stories of their own according to a systematic, step-by-step plan. In so doing, I am aware that *The Primer* runs the risks mentioned above. By insisting on a single, highly specific set of operations, I know that I am ruling out other possible approaches. But *The Primer*'s goal isn't to provide a survey of all possible ways of writing a story, it is to take beginning writers along the surest path to the completion of their first story. It's not The Way to write every story; it's A Way to start writing stories. Beginners who finish a first story according to *The Primer*'s system earn promotion to the rank of Story Writer, Grade 1, and are ready to try other storytelling techniques secure in the first-hand knowledge of how fiction works.

The Primer is designed to meet the needs of all beginning fiction writers, regardless of their circumstances. I have successfully used draft versions of it in my own college-level introductory classes for many years. A number of high school teachers have found it effective in junior- and senior-level courses. Participants in the annual Kansas State University Conference for High School Writers have followed a modified version of its method. But my fondest wish is that this book should be of use to writers with no one standing by ready to help them. Of course a tutorial book is always improved by having available a teacher or friend who understands its approach to talk over your problems with. But I hope that *The Primer* can stand completely on its own when necessary and give individual writers the help they need to develop their talents.

Flannery O'Connor once lamented that there were already too many would-be fiction writers around for the good of fiction writing. When I see the ever-rising flood of fiction submissions to the magazine I help to edit, and when I think of my own stories being subjected to this same increasingly competitive market, I can sympathize with Ms. O'Connor's plaint. Then I remember that I got into fishing only because of a spin-casting rig which made the basic operations of casting and line retrieval easy enough for me to manage as a beginner and still keep me interested in improving my technical skill. Had it not been for spin-casting, I would surely never have known the more refined pleasures of fly-casting. In that spirit, I encourage all who "feel the itch" to take up *The Primer* and write!

• one •

INTRODUCTION & PREWRITING

WHY WRITE STORIES?

Every book about fiction writing has to deal someplace with this question of the writer's motives. Readers of a how-to-do-it book like this need to feel sure before they start out that its author understands and respects their reasons for wanting to learn about story writing. In fact, whatever your motives for wishing to write fiction, they must be allowed. It is not for writers to defend writing. Rather, let those who would attack story writing prove their case. The question is not Why? but Why *not* write stories?

The human habit of storying is so bound up in human nature, we might as well ask, Why look at a sunset? or, Why listen to birds sing? It doesn't need justifying. It's simply one of the things we do. Oscar Wilde said we were the only creatures who blushed—or needed to. We're also the only ones who make up stories (or need to?). As for why we want—or need—to story, most likely it's because as a species humans tend to be more curious than cats. The narrator of Sherwood Anderson's short story says it for us all: "I want to know why."

While the rest of Earth's creatures seem content to take their lives pretty much as they come, we humans worry about proving our right to be here. We devise elaborate systems of belief (religion) and speculation (philosophy) about what our lives mean, we scrutinize the physical world to discover how it behaves (science) in hope of finding a clue to our part in it, and we create original works to celebrate and interpret its vitality, variety, and beauty (art). Storytelling is one of the forms art takes.

Storytellers make up stories as painters paint or potters pot, to express their creative ideas and send their message to anyone "out there" able to understand it. Like other artists, writers may try selling the fruits of their labors, but—also like other artists—they usually go on making artworks whether they sell them or not. So you might call it an addiction, an unbreakable habit, an irresistible compulsion. Those who do take it up with a view to getting rich quick usually find out even quicker that it is mighty demanding work for an uncertain wage. But it remains the drug of choice for thousands of underpaid creators all the same.

Now if this all seems to draw a dreary picture of the writer as some poor chump getting shoved around by forces beyond his control, it should be pointed out that most of these poor driven souls wouldn't swap their lot for any other. It really doesn't matter to most writers that they have to write. Most writers don't want to do something else. Regardless of pay, most fiction writers consider theirs to be the most satisfying job in the world. What do they have to be so smug about? Quite a lot, actually. For instance:

- Independence. Fiction writers are truly their own bosses. Since nobody can tell them what or when or even how to write, they have to self-start and self-sustain.
- Power. Fiction writers make things happen. Of course the lives they manipulate are imaginary, but this only means that those lives exist only as authors use their godlike power of invention to create them.
- Discovery. In probing the reasons for their invented characters' thoughts and behavior, writers broaden their understanding of human motivation at large and improve their comprehension of themselves. This self-knowledge may well be fiction writing's single greatest reward.
- Achievement. Above all else what keeps writers going is the prospect of crafting original artworks so fine as to be accepted as part of mankind's "permanent collection."

WHAT *THE PRIMER* PROMISES TO DO FOR YOU:

Follow *The Primer*'s series of lessons from start to finish and you'll end up writing an authentic, original short story. From "square one" all the way to a finished work of fiction, *The Primer* will guide your progress with clear instructions about what to do at each stage. No special literary skills or knowledge are needed. Technical terms are kept to a minimum, and those that are used are either clearly defined or their meanings are plain from their context. All you need bring along is your determination to write a short story and your willingness to keep applying your resources of memory and invention until you succeed.

You may feel you already know something about storytelling technique and so don't need to start at square one. But *The Primer* promises you a story only if you begin at the beginning and go forward without omitting a single step to the end. You will be following a complicated recipe with many ingredients and precise directions for measuring and mixing them. If you omit or modify any part of the process, you can easily spoil the end product. So set aside everything you feel you already know and start out with a completely open mind. If you find much of the first few lessons obvious and elementary, be careful that you don't read too fast. You could miss something essential.

In addition to learning one way of writing a story, you'll learn:

- how to know a short story from other literary forms by its shape and movement, and how to tell a good story from a bad one;
- how to apply the critical skills you'll learn in analyzing the good and bad points in your own writing;
- how to improve your story through revision.

WHAT *THE PRIMER* WON'T DO FOR YOU:

It won't work miracles. It's not magic. What you write will be a genuine short story, but not necessarily a great work of literature. You won't be changed into a literary genius, either. If you *are* a genius, your story will show it. But if you're an average person, you'll probably write an average story. Of course writing even an average story is something most people never do, so you will become a more exceptional person, regardless.

Another miracle it won't work is making publishers want to buy what you write. If you're more interested in *selling* fiction than in *writing* it, you really need a different book, something about marketing techniques and "product image enhancement strategies." This doesn't mean the story *The Primer* helps you write won't be valuable. It may even be salable. But these days even most salable short stories end up in low-budget literary magazines, rather than rich mass-circulation ones. Maybe the success of *Esquire*'s summer fiction special issues means that the big audience for good stories is still out there and the mass market for quality fiction is ready to stage a comeback.

In the meantime storytellers must go on cultivating their craft, knowing that the greatest pleasure really does come from feeling accomplishment within yourself rather than others' approval or payment. Samuel Johnson once said no one but a blockhead ever wrote except for money. In his gruff way he was telling writers to get their due like other professionals. But Johnson didn't mean that money was a writer's chief incentive. He didn't spend years doing the first English dictionary because he thought it would make him rich. It was truly a labor of love.

Your loyalty to personal standards should never be selfish. You don't live in a vacuum, and you can't write in one. You're a part of a society, and what you write must speak to that society if it's to mean anything. Always keep your audience in mind. Try to reach as many readers as you can. But make certain you're the first reader satisfied. To write only to please what you think is the crowd's taste is to give up your own convictions and disgrace your art.

KIPLING'S FIRST PRINCIPLES OF FICTION WRITING

The Victorian master storyteller Rudyard Kipling wrote: "There are nine and sixty ways of constructing tribal lays, and every single one of them is right." In a whimsical way Kipling made two essential points about fiction writing. First, there's no single best way to do it. Second, tribal lays—call them stories—are things that get "constructed."

The Primer describes only one of the "nine and sixty" *right* ways of building a story. Once you've done one or two using its method you'll be ready to try a different approach. You might start with a character. Charles Dickens said *The Pickwick Papers* came from his happening to imagine Mr. Pickwick. Joseph Conrad's creative imagination was once triggered simply by seeing a stranger descend a staircase. Perhaps you'll choose to begin with setting. For Robert Louis Stevenson stories lived like ghosts in certain old English country inns. Thomas Hardy's *The Return of the Native* started out with Egdon Heath, and the people came later. Or possibly, like Henry James, you'll begin with a theme or controlling idea—what he called his *donnee*, his "given." Most good stories seem to use a whole set of resources, and the wise writer stands ready to accept them in whatever shape or order they come, so long as they feed his creativity.

But that's for later, after you've done your first story according to *The Primer*'s directions. You can think of it as your reward for staying the course. But you may be wondering, if there are so many ways of writing a story, why make everyone go the same way? There's only one good answer to that question: *The Primer*'s way is closer to "fail safe" than any of the others. It's like following the least dangerous route to the top of a mountain. He who makes his first climb without breaking his neck lives to climb again—a harder route next time, maybe. But the first time what's important is making it all the way up. Which is what *The Primer* promises: to take you from the very base of this mountain all the way to its peak. And I guarantee the view from the top—every bit as fine as if you'd half killed yourself struggling up the north face. So make ready for a long but gradual ascent. It will be demanding, but not tedious. It will be exciting, as discovery is always exciting, and it will be positively thrilling in the end.

It sometimes bothers beginning fiction writers to be told that making a story is as demanding an experience as it is thrilling. Isn't creation supposed to be exciting, a kind of fireworks display of inspiration? No question about it, for the artist nothing beats the joy of creating an artwork. But as with any other craft, writing a story requires knowing the technique. If you don't have that, no amount of heart or mind will make your stories work. If you do, you can write effective, even publishable stories, even if your creative gift isn't huge.

Great stories are a combination of personal qualities and acquired technique. No book can provide the qualities, but *The Primer* will help you acquire the needed technique by getting you to write a real short story. It won't let you off with a sketch or vignette or mood piece or narrative essay or any other prose "whatyamacallit." If at any time you find your spirit sagging, just remember that what you're learning is the technical skill to make the most of whatever storytelling gift you have, to write the best stories you can.

The other point Kipling makes is equally important. *Stories are constructed things.* If they weren't, this whole book would be useless. If fiction is really something that gushes willy-nilly from the head of an "inspired" being, then all talk of technique is nonsense. The Inspiration School of creative writing doesn't believe in skill or craft. For them it's just a matter of picking up pennies from heaven, so good luck is more important than hard work. They think fiction is spilt, not built. To be sure, a story may sometimes almost seem to "write itself," and a few great authors have helped popularize the concept of inspiration. Coleridge said he conceived "Kubla Khan" in an opium trance, and Faulkner wanted us to believe that liquor made his creative juices flow. But the exceptions aren't the rule. Most great artists have been diligent, disciplined workers who proved the truth that "Genius is the infinite capacity for taking pains." Art is a planned product.

This doesn't mean that stories can be manufactured like cars on an assembly line. Many successful TV series may seem to have been put together from prefabricated pieces and to recycle the same old tired formulas over and over, but creativity really won't walk a treadmill. If a story works, whether sit-com, soap opera, or *The Brothers Karamazov*, it's because there's a live creative mind making it go. When Eudora Welty described a good story as a "continuing mystery," she didn't mean the sort of mystery a master sleuth tries to solve in a detective novel. What she meant was that you never get to the bottom of a good story because it always grows to keep pace with your own understanding.

The basic questions of life are never fully answered, so the subject matter of serious fiction is an ongoing challenge to story readers and writers alike. Just as the thrill of reading (and rereading) a good story comes from the depth of its "mystery," the thrill of writing fiction comes from investigating such mysteries in your own stories. Every practicing writer knows the joy of insight that can strike like lightning from a clear sky and the urge to shout "Eureka!" when that happens. Inspirationists say it's just more proof of the importance of luck. But artists know that they earn their luck.

The brilliant discovery happens because a seeking intelligence has been struggling to find a solution to a problem. Edison experimented with thousands of versions of the light bulb until the right combination flared into being. A flash always seems sudden no matter how long it is in coming. So for the fiction writer, "God helps him who helps himself" is a better motto than "The Lord will provide." The familiar cliché caricature of The Great Author sitting idly waiting for the spirit to move him is a false picture. Like other skilled craftsmen, writers have to work hard to put their ideas into words that combine in artistic ways.

WHERE EXACTLY IS SQUARE ONE?

The first step in writing a short story is to define what one is. Despite all the experimenting with fictional form in recent years, a short story is still basically just a detailed record of a few important events in an invented person's experience. If the record isn't detailed, it's a summary or a sketch. If the person's not invented (a "character"), it's biographical history. If there are more than a few events or several "main" characters, it's a novel. The events must be important for obvious reasons. You can't expect readers to sit still for *un*important events.

Imagine an individual life represented by a line graph passing through a series of daily segments. A typical day for most of us would get expressed by a flat line, because on most days nothing much happens, nothing terribly crucial. This isn't to say such typical days aren't enjoyable. Most of us don't like having our steady, peaceful routines disrupted by upheavals and crises. But sadly, good news is no news. It's not always easy staying interested in Aunt Grace's account of her afternoon shopping or even Grandpa's recollections of the "good old days." But at least we have our personal interest in them to help us through the dry parts of their stories. When the storyteller is a stranger talking about persons who are made-up characters, the story must have something exceptional about it to hold our attention.

So fiction concerns itself with those days when something does happen, when the line graph isn't flat because a "turning point" experience occurs to change things. This "deflection" can be expressed graphically by a crooked line.

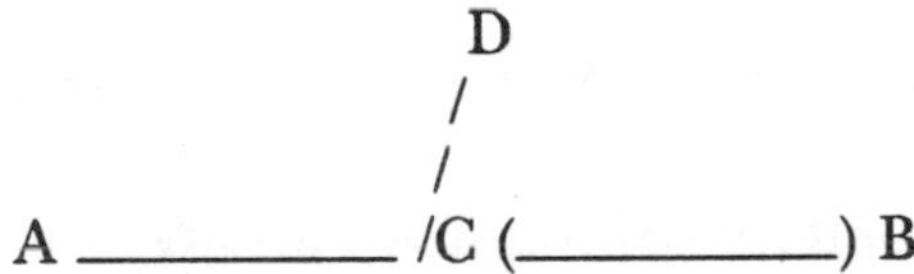

Our imaginary hero starts out his day at point A, possibly thinking to end it at point B (an ordinary day). But something happens at point C to change all that. So he ends his day at point D rather than point B. Whatever it was at point C, it had quite an impact and made a strong deflection in our hero's life line. Most of the best modern stories wouldn't show such an abrupt turn in their plots. They're more interested in seeming real than in being sensational. But no matter how quiet the action, there must always be a large enough crisis in the main character's life to cause a deflection that has meaning for the reader.

If we say that the primary *principle* of a short story is deflection, we can work out some of the main features of its *procedure* as well. First of all, readers ought to witness the actual turning-point crisis in full. Only if they share that experience with the main character, blow by blow, will they be able to appreciate how he or she feels about it. But they must know more than just the facts of the crisis itself. To understand events, we have to understand the context they occur in. This means, in a story, showing what led up to the crisis and what happened afterward as a result. The cause and the effect. The before and the after. In terms of our line graph it means taking at least three readings—at A, at C, and at D.

So a story is nothing more than a narrative account in three phases of a significant set of events in a fictitious person's life. If it's that simple, you may wonder why everybody isn't cranking them out. Because it's one thing to draw or photograph the Parthenon, something else to "invent" and build it. Still, if you want to design a beautiful temple, it's a good idea to study the plans of existing temples to learn how their architects' minds worked. In the same way, if you want to write stories, it pays to study examples of successful short fiction to try to see how their authors' minds arrived at such plans.

YOUR FIRST "WRITING" ASSIGNMENT

The starting point for writing your own first story isn't even writing. If you feel like protesting that you're being kept from work rather than put to work, just remember you're starting at square one. And square one in writing a story really is learning the feel of short story structure. Just think of this first assignment as a set of warm-up exercises to get you in shape before the big game. It might help to remind yourself that once you're through this one, every other assignment does require you to write.

Toward the end of the nineteenth century two great writers working in two very different countries and languages managed between them to pull together the various storytelling practices of their time, set up a basic structure for the short story, and lay down a few principles of fictional technique. These two masters of the "classic" (or "premodern") short story were Guy de Maupassant (1850-1893) and Anton Chekhov (1860-1904). We will examine a sample work by each of them and show how, despite their very different artistic personalities and goals, they wrote to the same structural rules. First, Maupassant. Read "The Jewels" below with a view to identifying its three component phases: exposition (beginning), complication/crisis (middle), and denouement (ending). Remember the basic definition of the short story given above, and all it implies. Spot the main character, identify the challenge to his status quo, note the moment and scope of his deflection and the nature of the resulting change in his attitude and situation.

The Jewels

(translation by Ben Nyberg)

M. Lantin having met this young woman at a soiree at the home of his assistant bureau chief, love enveloped him like a net.

She was the daughter of a provincial tax collector, dead some years past. She had come to Paris with her mother, who circulated among middle-class families in the neighborhood in the hope of marrying off her daughter. They were poor but respectable, quiet and gentle. The girl seemed the very perfection of true woman to whom a wise young man dreams of entrusting his life. Her modest beauty had the charm of angelic purity and the subtle smile which never left her lips seemed a reflection of her heart.

All the world sang her praises; all those who knew her never ceased repeating: "Happy he who gets her. One could never find better."

M. Lantin, then a principal clerk at the Ministry of the Interior with an annual salary of 3,500 francs, asked her to marry him, and she became his wife.

He was indescribably happy with her. She managed his house with so skillful an economy that they seemed to live in luxury. He lacked for no attention, no nicety, no delicacy which she might offer him; and the seductiveness of her personality was so great that six years after their meeting he loved her more than in the first days.

He found fault with only two of her tastes—that for the theater and that for fake jewelry.

Her friends (she knew several wives of minor functionaries) were always getting her box-seats for the latest hits, even first nights; and she dragged her husband willy-nilly to these entertainments, which utterly exhausted him after a hard day's work. So he begged her to consent to go to shows with some lady of her acquaintance who would see her home afterwards. For quite some time she refused to agree, finding it not a very proper arrangement. She decided at last to oblige him, and he was infinitely grateful.

Now this taste for theater soon nurtured in her a desire to

adorn herself. Her dresses remained entirely simple, it is true, always in good taste, however modest; and her sweet grace, her irresistible grace, humble and smiling, seemed to acquire a new savor from the simplicity of her gowns, but she took up the habit of wearing a pair of huge rhinestone earrings that looked like diamonds, a necklace of false pearls, bracelets of imitation gold, and combs ornamented with glass bits simulating fine stones.

Her husband, who was somewhat distressed by this love of ostentation, often remarked: "My dear, when people haven't the means to buy real jewels, they should display only the adornments of their beauty and their grace, which are ever the rarest gems."

But she would smile sweetly and reply: "What will you? I love them. They are my vice. I know you are right; but I can't remake myself. I would adore jewels, that I would!"

And she would roll the pearl necklace in her fingers, flash the facets of cut glass, saying: "Just look at how well it is made. You'd swear it was real."

He smiled, saying, "You have the tastes of a Bohemian."

Sometimes when they were spending the evening at home tête-à-tête by the fireplace, she would bring to their tea table the morocco case in which she secured her "junk," as her husband called it, and proceed to examine these imitation jewels with a passionate attention as if she savored some secret and profound pleasure; and she persisted in placing a necklace round her husband's throat, which made her laugh uncontrollably and cry out: "How droll you look!" Then she would throw herself into his arms and kiss him madly.

Having been to the opera one winter night, she returned all shivering with cold. Next day she was coughing. Eight days later she died of pneumonia.

Lantin almost followed her into the tomb. His despair was so terrible that his hair turned white in a month. He wept from morning to night, his spirit was rent with intolerable suffering, haunted by memory, by her smile, by her voice, by every charm of his dead wife.

Time did not lessen his grief. Often during his hours at the bureau when his colleagues would be chatting about topics of the day, his cheeks would suddenly swell, his nose wrinkle, his eyes fill with tears; he would make a frightful grimace and begin to weep.

He had kept his wife's room intact and shut himself up in it every day to think about her; and all the furniture and her clothing remained just as they had been left on her final day.

But life became hard for him. His salary, which in the hands of his wife had sufficed for all their needs, now became inadequate for him alone. And he asked himself with astonishment how she had managed to secure for him the superior wines and gourmet foods which he could no longer afford with his modest resources.

He fell into debt and ran about after money in the manner of those reduced to expedients. Finally one morning, as he found himself without a sou an entire week before the end of the month, he thought to sell something; and at once the idea came to him to dispose of his wife's "junk," because in the very bottom of his heart he felt a grudge against these counterfeits which had once vexed him. Their very sight each day marred the memory of his beloved.

It took a long time to sort through the pile of trinkets she had left behind, because to the end she had obstinately persisted in her collecting, coming home almost every evening with some new piece. He settled upon the grand necklace she seemed to prefer, which he thought might well fetch six or eight francs, it being so beautifully wrought, for an imitation.

He put it in his pocket and went his way toward the Ministry by way of the boulevards, searching for a jeweler's shop that looked trustworthy. At last he saw one and entered, a bit shamefaced at having to exhibit his poverty and try to sell a thing of so little worth.

"Monsieur," he said to the dealer, "I would appreciate knowing what value you place on this trifle."

The man took the object, examined it, turned it over, weighed it, put it under a magnifying glass, called to his clerk, spoke in low tones to him, placed the necklace on his counter and studied it at a distance to better judge its effect.

M. Lantin, agitated by all these ceremonies, opened his mouth to declare "Oh I know that they're of no value" when the jeweler said:

"Monsieur, this is worth between twelve and fifteen thousand francs; but I cannot buy it from you unless you can tell me exactly how you obtained it."

The widower opened his eyes wide and stood gaping, not comprehending. At length he stammered, "What do you say? Are you sure?" The other misinterpreted his astonishment and said in a dry voice: "You can ask around if you think you can do better. To me it is worth at most fifteen thousand. You may come back here if you find you can't do better."

M. Lantin, totally bewildered, took the necklace and departed, sensing a confused need to be alone and to think.

But as soon as he was in the street, he felt more like laughing. "The fool," he thought. "Oh, the fool! I might have taken him at his word, all the same. That's some jeweler who can't tell false gems from real ones!"

And he went into another shop at the beginning of the Rue de la Paix. No sooner had the dealer seen the necklace than he exclaimed: "Ah *parbleu*! I know it well, this piece. It came from my shop."

Deeply troubled, M. Lantin asked, "What is it worth?"

"Monsieur, I sold it for twenty-five thousand. I am prepared to take it back for eighteen thousand, upon your establishing—as the law requires—how it came into your possession."

At this M. Lantin sat down, stiff with astonishment. He went on: "But ... but, examine it closely, monsieur. Till just now I have believed it was . . . paste."

The jeweler replied, "Would you give me your name, monsieur?"

"Of course. My name is Lantin. I am employed in the Ministry of the Interior. I live at 16 Rue des Martyrs."

The merchant opened his register, searched it, and declared: "The necklace was sent to Mme. Lantin, 16 Rue des Martyrs, 20 July, 1876."

And the two men looked into each other's eyes, the widower stunned by shock, the jeweler scenting a thief.

The latter finally spoke: "Will you leave this necklace with me for twenty-four hours? I can give you a receipt."

M. Lantin stammered, "Of course, certainly." And he went off, folding the bit of paper and putting it in his pocket.

Then he crossed the street, went back, saw that he had mistaken his route, returned to the Tuileries, crossed the Seine, realized he was in error again, and regained the Champs Elysees without a clear notion in his head. He did his best to think, to understand. His wife could not have bought an article of such value. That was certain. But then it had to have been a gift. A present! But a present from whom? For what?

He stopped and stood motionless in the middle of the avenue. A horrible suspicion dawned on him. She? But then all the other gems must have been gifts too. It seemed to him that the ground trembled, that a tree in front of him bent over; he thrust out his arms and fell in a faint.

He regained consciousness in a pharmacist's shop to which passersby had carried him. He had himself taken home and there shut himself in.

Till nightfall he wept violently, biting a handkerchief so as not to cry out. Then he put himself to bed, worn out with fatigue and sorrow, and fell into a heavy sleep.

A ray of sunshine woke him, and he rose reluctantly to go to his office. It would be hard to work after such a shock. He thought then that he might excuse himself to his superior, and he wrote to him. Then he remembered that he had to return to the jeweler's, and he blushed with shame. He paused a long time to consider. He could not leave the necklace at that man's shop, so he dressed and went out.

It was a lovely day, blue sky spread out over a smiling city. The dandies strolled idly, hands in pockets.

Lantin told himself as he watched them pass, "How happy you can be if you are wealthy. With money you can shake off even grief, go where you like, travel, divert yourself. Oh, if I were rich!"

He discovered that he was hungry, having eaten nothing for two days. But his pockets were empty, and he recalled the necklace. Eighteen thousand francs. Quite a sum, that!

He reached the Rue de la Paix and began walking back and forth on the sidewalk opposite the shop. Eighteen thousand francs! Twenty times he was on the point of entering, but his shame always held him back.

He was hungry, though, very hungry, and hadn't a sou. Abruptly he made up his mind, crossed the street running, so as to allow no time for reflection, and flung himself into the dealer's shop.

As soon as he saw Lantin, the merchant came forward eagerly, offered a chair with smiling politeness. The clerks also appeared, observing the customer from one side with amusement in their eyes and on their lips.

The jeweler said, "I have made inquiries, monsieur, and if you are still of the same mind, I am ready to pay you the agreed sum."

The poor man sputtered, "But of course . . ."

The dealer took from a drawer eighteen large notes, counted them, handed them to Lantin, who signed a small receipt and with a shaky hand put the money in his pocket.

Then as he prepared to leave, he turned back to the owner, who was still smiling, and spoke with lowered eyes: "I have . . . have other jewels . . . which came to me . . . in the same inheritance. Would you wish to buy them from me as well?"

The merchant bowed. "But of course, monsieur." One of the clerks left so as to laugh at his ease; the other blew his nose loudly.

Lantin, impassive, flushed and grave, said: "I shall bring them to you."

And he took a hackney cab to go collect his happiness.

When he returned to the shop an hour later he still had not eaten. They set to examining the objects piece by piece, appraising each. Nearly all of them had come from this supplier.

Lantin now haggled over the valuations, got angry, demanded to be shown the sales register, and spoke more and more loudly in proportion as the total rose.

The large diamond earrings were worth twenty thousand francs; the bracelets, thirty-five thousand; the brooches, rings, and lockets, sixteen thousand; a necklace of emeralds and sapphires, fourteen thousand; a solitaire pendant on a chain of gold, forty thousand; the whole reaching the figure of 196,000 francs.

The merchant declared with good-natured raillery: "This was a person who put every bit of savings into jewelry."

Lantin rejoined solemnly: "It is one way, like another, of investing money." And he went off, having agreed with the buyer that a second expert valuation be conducted the following day.

When he found himself back in the street, he eyed the Vendome Column aching to scale it like a greased pole. He felt light enough to leapfrog over the Emperor's statue perched up there in the sky.

He had lunch at Voisin's and drank wine at twenty francs a bottle. Then he hired a coach and took a drive round the Bois. He regarded the carriages with a certain scorn, restraining his urge to cry out to the passersby, "I too am rich. I have two hundred thousand francs!"

The thought of his office occurred to him. He had himself driven there, entered the bureau chief's office resolutely and announced: "I come, monsieur, to submit my resignation. I have inherited 300,000 francs." He went round shaking hands with his former colleagues and treating them to some of his plans for his new life. Then he dined at the Cafe Anglais.

Finding himself seated beside a gentleman who appeared to

be distinguished, he could not help confiding in him, with an air of coyness, that he had come into an inheritance of 400,000 francs.

For the first time in his life he was not bored by the theater, and he spent the evening in the company of young women.

Six months later he remarried. His second wife was totally respectable, but of a difficult disposition. She caused him much suffering.

A Maupassantian short story is usually an ironic moral fable that shows how seemingly trivial events can bring great changes in ordinary people's lives. Human beings have little control over their lives, which are manipulated by the accidents of fate. Its plot is normally a clearly charted sequence of surprising, often coincidental turns, which bend characters' lives into striking thematic patterns. Narrative tone is normally detached, journalistic, sometimes slightly cynical. The workings of characters' minds are presented only as needed to show the influence of external factors on their motives and behavior.

With his usual plainness and directness, Maupassant thrusts the name of his main character at us straightaway in the story's first sentence: "M[onsieur] Lantin having met this young woman at a soiree at the home of his assistant bureau chief, love enveloped him like a net." Attention, Maupassant says, I want to tell you a story about some jewels and a man named Lantin.

Having located our main character with no difficulty, we must follow him to find out "what happens" to him. By the end of the first sentence, he is already in love. Within four paragraphs, he is married. Six years pass in a single paragraph, leaving him more in love with his wife than ever. Well and good, but clearly all part of the setup, the calm before the storm.

Then comes the first ripple of disquiet: "He found fault with only two of her tastes—that for the theater and that for fake jewelry." We take note of this clue, keep it handy for use when the developing puzzle is ready to receive it. But our story is still in its opening, expository phase where the stage is being set for future events. Nothing unusual or particular has actually "happened" to our character. Several paragraphs follow in which Maupassant recounts background incidents from the Lantins' life together that will help readers appreciate the crisis about to be described.

Finally, in a short three-sentence paragraph, the joy of Lantin's life is snuffed out—his "perfect" wife dies. At last the story's crisis has arrived, right? Not exactly. What has arrived is the event that precipitates the crisis. The exposition is over; the crucial middle phase has begun. But though Lantin is emotionally shattered by the death of his wife, his feeling for her actually stays the same. If this were the sum of Maupassant's idea—a man, happily married to an almost faultless woman, is devastated by her sudden death—the story would lack both bite and pith. It would seem a paltry sort of story, flat and obvious. Until a character is somehow challenged by developments in his life, his existence lacks fictional significance.

So Lantin is laid low by his loss, but his belief in his wife as a flawless paragon remains unchanged. She stays on her pedestal, he obsessively worships her memory. Then once again, Maupassant drops a hint for us to ponder: "His salary, which in the hands of his wife had sufficed for all their needs, now became inadequate for him alone." Not only a clue for the reader, but a goad that prods Lantin one step closer to his discovery.

Desperate for money, he is reduced to searching among his wife's gewgaws for something to sell. When he takes the necklace to the jeweler and learns that the gems are real, his own values are at last seriously challenged. His belief in the purity and simplicity of his wife's character is shaken, as the possible meaning of all her costly gifts begins to sink in. In a subtle paragraph, Maupassant depicts his bewilderment:

> Then he crossed the street, went back, saw that he had mistaken his route, returned to the Tuileries, crossed the Seine, realized he was in error again, and regained the Champs-Elysees without a single clear notion in his head.

When the truth finally dawns, he falls in a swoon, completely overcome. But by the next day, Maupassant sets the mood for a change: "A ray of sunshine woke him." He feels shame, of course, but soon he thinks: "How happy you can be if you are wealthy. With money you can shake off even grief . . ." Already he is preparing himself mentally to profit from his new discovery. Penniless and hungry, he paces a while outside the jeweler's. But not for long: "He . . . crossed the street running, so as to allow no time for reflection, and flung himself into the dealer's shop."

With this act, Lantin shows that his attitude has changed. In deciding to profit from his dead wife's jewels, he gives up any right he might have had to feel morally superior to her. His neglectful "love" had survived six years of marriage, his misguided worship of her memory many months; his self-righteous shame lasts only a day. At the point when he decides to cash in on his wife's "favors" by selling the jewels, he truly accepts both as his own, and the crucial middle phase of the story is over.

Having traded in his innocence for cynicism, he turns shrewd very quickly: "Lantin now haggled over the valuations, got angry, demanded to be shown the sales register, and spoke more and more loudly in proportion as the total rose." His bickering brings its reward: 196,000 francs. But when he leaves the jeweler's shop, though his need has been met, his greed continues to grow. As he rides round the Bois de Boulogne, he rounds the figure of his new fortune up to 200,000 francs. By the time he resigns from his job he has inflated his "inheritance" to 300,000. Later that day he boasts of 400,000 francs. His wealth has truly gone to his head.

Maupassant saves back a two-pronged stinger to close with: "For the first time in his life he [Lantin] was not bored by the theater and spent the evening in the company of young women." He has adopted his wife's tastes along with her resources.

Then, to complete the circle, "Six months later he remarried. His second wife was totally respectable, but of a difficult disposition. She caused him much suffering." Lantin was apparently looking to avoid in his second marriage the hazards of his first, but also escaped its joys. Perhaps a vestige of his conscience remains alive to keep him from fully enjoying his first wife's "ill gotten gains." Maupassant doesn't explore the why, simply noting the irony and letting us draw our own conclusions.

The mode and intent of Anton Chekhov differ widely from those of Maupassant. Only ten years separate the two masters, but they are worlds apart in attitude and technique. Where

Maupassant was fatalistic, Chekhov felt humans made real choices and deserved the credit, or discredit, for their achievements, good or bad. This fundamental difference in outlook affects the structure of their stories.

Because Maupassant sees people as pawns pushed along by outside forces, he lays heavy emphasis on plot and setting. Chekhov focuses his attention on how and why individuals make the decisions they do, so naturally he spends more time exploring character. He records his characters' thoughts in detail and tends to quote their statements directly rather than paraphrasing, as Maupassant prefers. Theme is important to both, but Maupassant's theme tends to remain the same—that hereditary and environmental factors control human behavior—whereas Chekhov's themes are as varied as the characters he represents. A Chekhov story often contains ironies, but unlike one by Maupassant the irony is not usually the sole or final point of the narrative.

Read the Chekhov story, "Turmoil," printed below. Identify the main character and observe how her reactions and decisions arise from her qualities as an individual rather than a type. Decide where you feel the lines between the three phases should be drawn, where the deflection happens, and what change occurs.

Turmoil

(translation by F. D. Reeve)

Mashenka Pavletskaya, a pretty young woman who had only recently graduated from finishing school, after a walk returned to the Kushkins', where she was the governess, to find the place in an uproar. Mikhailo, the porter who opened the door for her, was as agitated and red as a lobster.

Upstairs there was a terrible commotion.

"Probably Madam has had a nervous fit," Mashenka thought, "or gotten into a fight with her husband."

In the vestibule and in the hallway she ran into some of the maids. One was crying. Then Mashenka saw her master, Nikolai Sergeich, dash out of her own room—a short man, decidedly middle-aged with a flabby face and a big bald patch. His face was red, and all twisted. Without noticing the governess, he shot past hands in the air, and cried out, "Oh, it's awful! So tactless! So stupid! Mad! Foul!"

Mashenka went on into her room and, for the first time in her life, felt the full force of what all those feel who meekly depend for their livelihood on service to the rich and well-born. Her room was being searched. Fedosya Vasilyevna, her mistress, a dumpy, broad-shouldered lady with thick black brows, hatless and awkward, with a trace of a moustache and red hands, her face and manners those of a plain country cook, was standing at her work table and stuffing back into her bag balls of yarn, scraps of material, little pieces of paper. Clearly the governess's appearance surprised her; so, looking up and noticing her pale, astonished expression, she was a little embarrassed and muttered:

"*Pardon*, I—I knocked it over—My sleeve caught it."

Mumbling something else and swishing her skirt around her, Madam Kushkin went out. With eyes of wonder, Mashenka looked around her room and, understanding nothing, not knowing what to make of it, shrugged and shivered in fear. What was Fedosya Vasilyevna looking for in her bag? If, as she said, she really had caught it with her sleeve and upset it, then why had Nikolai Sergeich run out of the room so red-faced and agitated? Why did one drawer of the table stick slightly out? The moneybox in which she kept small change and old stamps lay open. Someone had opened it but couldn't get it closed although they had completely scratched up the lock. The bookstand, the table top, the bed—all bore fresh signs of the search. Even the linen basket. Her things were carefully folded but not in the order Mashenka had left them when she went out. The search had certainly been thorough, as thorough as possible, but why? what for? What had happened? Mashenka remembered the porter's nervousness, the turmoil still going on, the maid's tear-stained face—didn't all that have some connection with the search that had just taken place in her room? Was she involved in some dreadful affair? Mashenka paled and, turning ice cold, sank down on the linen basket.

A maid came in.

"Liza, you don't happen to know why I—was searched?" the governess asked her.

"Madam has lost a brooch worth two thousand," Liza said.

"But why search me?"

"They searched everyone, Miss. They turned me inside-out. They stripped us naked and searched us. And I swear to God,

Miss, never mind a brooch, I haven't been near her dressing table. And I'll say so to the police, too."

"But why search me?" the young governess continued incredulously.

"Like I say, a brooch was stolen. Madam herself ransacked everything with her own hands. Herself personally searched even Mikhailo the porter. It's a downright disgrace! Nikolai Sergeich just looks on and clucks like a chicken. But you, Miss, have got nothing to be afraid about. They didn't find nothing in your room! Seeing as you didn't take the brooch, you've got nothing to be scared of."

"But, Liza, it's so underhanded—so humiliating!" said Mashenka, gasping in indignation. "It's such a dirty thing to do, so low! What right did she have to suspect me and rummage through my things?"

"You're not with your own family, Miss," said Liza with a sigh. "Even if you're a young lady, and everything, still—you're a kind of servant. It's not like living with Mummy and Daddy."

Mashenka crumpled onto her bed and began weeping bitterly. Such violence had never before been visited on her; never before had she been so deeply humiliated. She, a well-brought-up, sensitive young woman, a teacher's daughter, had been suspected of theft, and searched like a streetwalker. There could be no greater humiliation. And on top of the insult there was the worrisome fear of what would be next. If they could suspect her of theft, then they could now arrest her, strip her, search her, march her through the streets under guard, lock her up in a dark, cold cell with mice and wood lice, exactly like the young Princess Tarakanova. Who would stand up for her? Her parents were far away in the country, hadn't the money to come see her. She was alone in the capital as if in a barren field, without family or friends. They could do with her whatever they wanted.

"I'll run to all the lawyers and judges," Mashenka thought, trembling, "explain to them, take an oath—and they'll see that I can't be a thief."

Mashenka remembered that under the sheets in her linen basket lay some sweetmeats that out of old school habit she had slipped into her pocket during dinner and taken back to her room. The idea that her little secret was now known to her employers threw her into a fever, filled her with shame, and because of everything—the fear, the shame, and the grievance—her heart started pounding in her temples, in her hands, all through her insides

"Dinner's ready!"

Mashenka was called. "To go or not to?"

Mashenka fixed her hair, wiped her face with a moist towel and went to the dining room. There they had begun eating. Fedosya Vasilyevna sat at one end of the table, full of importance, her face black and serious; at the other end was Nikolai Sergeich. Along the sides were the guests and children. Dinner was being served by two footmen in tailcoats and white gloves. Everyone knew that the house was in turmoil, that the Madam was depressed, and they kept quiet. The only sounds were people's chewing and the spoons tapping the soup plates.

Madam herself began the conversation.

"What's the entree?" she asked one of the footmen in a long-suffering voice.

"*L'esturgeon a la russe,*" the footman replied.

"I ordered that, Fenya," Nikolai Sergeich quickly put in. "Wanted a little fish. If you don't like it, *ma chere*, tell them not to serve it. I was just—and besides—"

Fedosya Vasilyevna didn't like dishes she hadn't ordered herself, and now her eyes filled with tears.

"Ooh, let's not get upset," said Mamikov, her house doctor, in a saccharine voice, lightly touching her arm and smiling as saccharinely. "As it is, we're upset enough. Let's forget about the brooch! Health is worth more than two thousand."

"I don't care about the two thousand!" replied the hostess, and a big tear ran down her cheek. "It's the fact that it happened makes me indignant! I won't have thieves in my house! It's not the money, I don't care about any of the things, but to steal from me—what ingratitude! After all my kindness, to be repaid like that—"

Everyone was looking down at his plate, but Mashenka thought that, after what the Madam said, everyone glanced at her. A lump suddenly rose in her throat, she started crying and pressed her handkerchief to her face.

"*Pardon,*" she mumbled. "It's too much for me. I have a headache. Excuse me."

She rose from the table, awkwardly scraping her chair on the floor and behaving even more embarrassedly, and quickly left.

"God knows what's happening!" said Nikolai Sergeich frowning. "Some need there was to search her room! That really was—unfortunate."

"I'm not saying she took the brooch," said Fedosya Vasilyevna, "but can you vouch for her? I have to admit I don't set much store by these poor, well-educated young things."

"Really, Fenya, unfortunate. Excuse me, Fenya, but legally you have no right to conduct searches."

"I know nothing about your laws. All I know is that I lost a brooch. And I'm going to find it!" She struck her plate with her fork, and her eyes sparkled with fury. "You keep eating and mind your own business!"

Nikolai Sergeich meekly looked down and sighed. Meanwhile, back in her room, Mashenka had crumpled onto her bed. She was no longer either afraid or ashamed but tormented by an almost overpowering desire to go and slap that callous, arrogant, stupid, lucky woman.

Lying there, she breathed into her pillow and dreamed how great it would be to go buy the most expensive brooch there was and throw it in that petty tyrant's face. Or if only God would grant it, Fedosya Vasilyevna would be ruined, she'd have to become a beggar and would understand the whole horror of being poor and dependent, and the once-humiliated Mashenka would give her alms! Oh, suddenly to inherit a fortune and buy a carriage and noisily drive past under her windows, so that she was filled with envy!

All this was a dream; in real life, there was only one thing to do—to leave as soon as possible, not to remain another hour. To be sure, losing the position was frightening, to have to return to her parents, who had nothing, but what could she do? Mashenka could no longer stand the thought of the Madam or of her own little eerie, stifling room. Fedosya Vasilyevna, neurotic about illnesses and her imagined aristocratic nature, was so repugnant to her that the whole world seemed vulgar and unsightly because this woman was alive. Mashenka jumped up and started packing.

"May I come in?" Nikolai Sergeich asked from the hallway. He had come to the door unheard, and he spoke softly. "May I?"

"Come in."

He came in and stopped by the door. His eyes were dulled, and the tip of his nose was red and shiny. He had been drinking beer after dinner, made clear by the way he walked and loosely, passively held his hands.

"What's this mean?" he asked, pointing to the basket.

"I'm packing. Forgive me, Nikolai Sergeich, but I can't remain in your house. This search has deeply offended me."

"I understand. Only, you're making a mistake to—What for?

Your room was searched, and so you—what difference does it make to you? Nothing's going to happen to you."

Mashenka said nothing and kept on packing. Nikolai Sergeich tweaked his moustache as if pondering what else to say and continued in an ingratiating tone:

" 'course I understand, but you have to be tolerant. My wife, you know, is high-strung, eccentric, mustn't be judged harshly—" Mashenka said nothing. "If you're really so offended," Nikolai Sergeich went on, "please accept apologies from me. My apologies."

Mashenka made no reply but only bent lower over her suitcase. This indecisive drunk was of absolutely no significance in the house. He played the pathetic role of sponger and superfluous man even with a servant, and his apology, too, signified absolutely nothing.

"Hm. Not a word? Not far enough for you? Well, then, I apologize for my wife. On behalf of my wife—she behaved tactlessly, I admit, like a nobleman—" Nikolai Sergeich paced back and forth, sighed and continued, "So what you want is to drive it in, right into my heart—You want my conscience to torture me—"

"I know you're not to blame, Nikolai Sergeich," Mashenka said, looking straight at him with her big, tear-stained eyes. "Why should it bother you?"

"Naturally—But still you're not right—don't go. Please." Mashenka shook her head. Nikolai Sergeich paused at the window and drummed on a pane. "For me misunderstandings like this are pure torture," he continued. "What should I do—fall on my knees before you, is that it? Your pride has been offended, and so you've shed tears, and you're packing up to leave, but you know, I have my pride, too, but you're not thinking about that. You want me to tell you what I wouldn't confess to a priest? That what you want? Listen here: you want me to admit what I'll never confess to my dying day?" Mashenka said nothing. "I took my wife's brooch!" Nikolai Sergeich said quickly. "Now you pleased? satisfied? Yes, I—took it—only, of course, I'm relying on your reticence. For God's sake, not a word to anyone, not a hint!"

Astonished and frightened, Mashenka kept on packing, grabbing her things, rumpling them and stuffing them into her suitcase and basket. Now, after Nikolai Sergeich's frank confession, she couldn't remain another minute and didn't see how she had ever been able to stand living in this house.

"Nothing to be surprised at," Nikolai Sergeich continued after a brief silence. "A common story! I need money, and she—won't let me have any. My father acquired this house and the whole place, you know, Marya Andreyevna! It's all mine, see, and the brooch was my mother's, and—everything's mine! But she took it over, took control of everything. No way I can take her to court, agreed. Please, I earnestly beseech you, accept my apologies—and stay here. *Tout comprendre, tout pardonner.* Won't you stay?"

"No!" said Mashenka firmly, beginning to tremble. "Leave me alone, I beg you."

"Well, no matter." Nikolai Sergeich sighed and sat down on the stool beside the suitcase. "Must admit I like people who can still be offended, hold others in contempt, and so on. I could sit here forever and look at your indignant expression. So, you really won't stay? I understand. Can't be otherwise. Sure. It comes out bad for you, but for me—oh, brmmmm! Can't set a foot out of this cellar. Go over to another of our estates, say, and I'm surrounded by my wife's scoundrelly relatives—the managers, the agronomists—the hell with them all. They slip something behind their backs, keep piling it up. No fish to catch, no grass to walk on, no trees to break a branch off of."

"Nikolai Sergeich!" Fedosya Vasilyevna's voice rang out in the hall. "Agniya, call your master!"

"So you're not staying?" Nikolai Sergeich asked, quickly rising and going to the door. "Because you could, honestly. I'd drop in in the evening, and we'd have a little chat. Hunh? Stay! If you go, there won't be a single human being left in the house. It's horrible!"

Nikolai Sergeich's pale, haggard expression was pleading, but Mashenka shook her head, and he, with a dismissive wave of his hand, went out.

A half hour later she was on her way.

Like Maupassant in "The Jewels," Chekhov makes no secret of who the main character is: "Mashenka Pavletskaya, a pretty young woman who had only recently graduated from finishing school," the story begins, focusing our attention at once upon Mashenka. It is her experience that we are about to witness, and it will be from her vantage point that we watch it unfold. By explicitly quoting her thought, "Probably Madam has had a nervous fit or gotten into a fight with her husband," Chekhov signals his intent to reveal Mashenka's reactions as well.

When she enters her room, we learn that her feelings are going to help us understand and interpret whatever happens: "... for the first time in her life, [she] felt the full force of what all those feel who meekly depend for their livelihood on service to the rich and well-born." Chekhov's attitude toward Mashenka is clearly sympathetic. He believes she is being ill-used and wants us to share this view. To encourage us, he describes the "rich and well-born" mistress of the house: "a dumpy, broad-shouldered lady with thick black brows, hatless and awkward, with a trace of a moustache, and red hands, her face and manners those of a plain country cook . . ."

It may seem at first that the crisis of the story is upon Mashenka before the exposition can be presented, but in fact Chekhov is only doing a good job of keeping the exposition dramatic. We find that a search is under way for a missing brooch. Mashenka cannot believe that she is included among the suspects and asks Liza repeatedly why the privacy of her room has been violated. Liza says everyone is suspected, but reassures Mashenka: "they didn't find nothing in your room! Seeing as you didn't take the brooch, you've nothing to be scared of." Of course this is a fresh insult to Mashenka's naive innocence, and she drops onto her bed to weep over her hopeless grief.

So now the full measure of her feelings of degradation have been defined, and the exposition is concluded? Almost. As she lies there brooding on her wrongs, she recalls some sweetmeats she has hidden away in her basket under the sheets, and feels hot with fresh shame. That the horrid, vulgar mistress of the house should have discovered this petty breach of good breeding on her own part brings her cup of bitterness to its brim.

Having established the extent of the affront to Mashenka's honor, our story proceeds to its crisis—the testing of Mashenka's spirit. Dinner is announced, and Mashenka asks herself whether she should go or not. Apparently she decides not to be intimidated, and sets about making herself presentable. But the mood in the dining room is strained, and soon Madam Kushkin begins to complain about the theft and how it repays all her kindness with ingratitude. This seems so clearly directed at the dependent Mashenka that she excuses herself and goes back to her room.

A series of exchanges follow between Madam Kushkin and her husband Nikolai that, technically speaking, violate the story's point of view, since Mashenka isn't there to hear them. But because they neither conceal nor reveal anything essential to Mashenka's understanding of her situation, and because they are so brief that we don't really lose touch with Mashenka while she is "off stage," the violation seems not to damage the story in any way, and in fact gives the reader a passing glimpse at Nikolai that will prove helpful later.

Significantly, on reentering her room Mashenka once again falls onto her bed, only this time she is "no longer either afraid or ashamed but tormented by an almost overpowering desire to go and slap that callous, arrogant, stupid, lucky woman." That's the spirit, Mashenka, we cheer. Go to it!

Only of course we know she can't realistically take on the entire corrupt social system on her own. She can't actually knock the awful woman's block off. But we want her to "speak up" in some fashion, to show her feelings strongly and clearly in a definite gesture of defiance. Mashenka's overheated teenage mind runs over a number of wishes before settling on the obvious right course to take: "to leave as soon as possible, not to remain another hour." Having reached this conclusion, Mashenka begins packing. The second phase of the story is finished.

Phase three begins with the arrival of Nikolai at her door. He asks her not to go, making a variety of excuses until finally he admits that he himself stole the brooch. Mashenka is astonished and frightened by this confession, which only adds to her distress, and causes her to hasten her packing, "grabbing her things, rumpling them and stuffing them into her suitcase and basket." But Nikolai, having spilled so much, plunges shamelessly ahead: "My father acquired this house and the whole place, you know, Marya Andreyevna! It's all mine, see, and the brooch was my mother's, and—everything's mine! But she took it over, took control of everything . . . I earnestly beseech you, accept my apologies—and stay here. *Tout comprendre, tout pardonner.* [To understand all is to forgive all.] Won't you stay?"

Mashenka remains resolute, confirming her earlier determination, and Nikolai can only admire her grit: "Must admit I like people who can still be offended, hold others in contempt, and so on. I could sit here forever and look at your indignant expression." He makes one last appeal for pity: "If you go, there won't be a single human being left in the house." But she must go: "A half hour later she was on her way."

The three-phase demonstration is complete. A sensitive young woman is subjected to a severe test of her self-esteem; the question is, will she submit to some humiliation in order to hold onto the security of her position? Her answer—and Chekhov seems to think it the right answer—is that no position can be worth keeping that degrades or debases her opinion of herself. It takes some quick growing up on her part, but she adapts effectively to meet the challenge.

Maupassant and Chekhov set the mode of the short story written from the 1880s up to World War I, the "premodern" story that seems to peak in the elaborate masterworks of Henry James. But a new wave of experimentation had already begun. In *Dubliners* (1914) James Joyce gave up conventional resolutions in favor of "epiphanies" (sudden manifestations or perceptions of the meaning of something); and in the early 1920s Sherwood Anderson brought his "slice of life" approach to storytelling. These new "modern" short stories looked strange to many readers. Some felt that Ernest Hemingway (1899-1961) radically redesigned the basic form of short fiction.

But of course the change couldn't really be that drastic. For a story to work, it had to do certain fundamental things. You might disguise it by trying to make it seem "true" rather than "made up," but it still needed three phases of development, a crisis and a deflection, a feeling of significance. Printed below is a fair sample of the kind of "modern" story being written today. See if you can sort out its main character, three phases, crisis, deflection, and thematic point. Don't be dismayed if you can't make as certain sense of it as you did of the Maupassant and Chekhov stories.

The Reasonable Request

Sally V. Doud

It seemed at first to be an impulse. There was no reason for the walk.

"A great idea," Mike had said on the phone.

She told him, "Yeah, well it's raining." She made it sound wet.

"So what?" he said. "Perfect night for a walk in the rain."

"Is it all right?"

"Sure," he said.

"You won't have any trouble?"

"No one will find out," he said. "No one will even notice."

The child was already in bed and had been asleep for a while. The door to its room was open a crack but there was no sound.

"I guess so," she said. "But not too long."

"Don't force yourself."

She said, "Once around the block."

It sounded fine.

They parked the car near a restaurant called after a famous movie star who died and left his name to the public. Mike got out, erected the umbrella and opened her door. She came up under his umbrella.

Across the street couples were hurrying toward the restaurant. The rain fell in a mist, so fine it made no sound on the umbrella. A police car slickered by.

As they started along the street she held on to his arm. She tried to recall a film she'd been to see a long time ago where the people walked around in the rain. There were probably thousands of films like that; it was something to do in a film but not in real life. In real life rain made people plunge and curse. But not the two of them, not tonight.

Another couple hurried by in the opposite direction with their heads held down against the mist. The night streets held the sound close. They might be invisible walking.

He said, "What is it?"

"You're not supposed to be seen with me," she said.

"Oh who cares," he said. "I don't care any more. Do you?"

She laughed. "Let 'em see. Nobody knows where we are. Wherever we might be expected to be, no one could possibly expect us to be here, right now." She let go of his arm.

He tried to put his arm around her but she shrugged it away.

"Why did you come?" he said.

"Because you asked me to. I suppose."

"No. Really why?"

"That's it."

"That's it?" He almost stopped walking.

"What do you want?"

He said, "That's not much of a reason."

They turned the first corner. This part of the block was dark, away from the street lamps. The houses were set farther back from the sidewalk.

"What do you want me to say?"

"I guess anyone would like to believe you came because of them—"

"I came because you asked," she repeated. "Isn't that enough?"

"You could have said no."

"Not really."

"God! you make it sound like you had no choice. Anyone can say no."

She said, "Maybe I should have. But I'm here now."

He was rubbing his other hand up and down the shaft of the umbrella handle. "Well, then it throws it back onto me to make any sense of it. Anybody can ask you something and you have to respond one way or the other. But in the end you have to be able to make sense of it."

She did not want to tell him how he was acting. She said, "I don't know why you always feel you have to make sense of everything."

"It's an obligation. I feel a personal responsibility to find the rational answer. Everyone does really. To make the connection."

They had turned the second corner. It was much lighter. All sorts of details appeared. Cracks in the sidewalk, door knockers, wet fallen leaves.

"I don't," she said. "What kind of connection?" They really didn't need to be under an umbrella; her hair was so wet it hung dripping against her shoulders. She held her hand out from under its protection to see if there was any difference. Very little.

"The relationship," he was still saying, "between question and answer. To understand them."

"What a subject!" she said. "What a place for a subject."

"Would you rather have a beer?" He named the restaurant.

"It wouldn't be walking in the rain."

"We don't have to," he said.

"That's what you called me for, wasn't it?"

She became aware of a man who seemed to have detached himself from the rest of the world and was following them. Except for his face caved in under a flat cap, he was grey and formless in an oversized coat. He carried no umbrella and must be soggy.

"Mike," she said, "look back at the man behind us."

Mike groaned. "He'll want a handout." The man hurried to catch up to them now that he was noticed.

She didn't really want to stop. The cadence would be broken. The man came up close and said something to Mike in a low voice she couldn't hear.

"What did he say?" she asked. "What does he want?" She felt she had a right to hear it herself. As long as they had to stop.

Mike said, "He says we have to go into this alley up here."

"Get in the alley," the man said loud enough for her to hear, "or I'll blow your brains out."

Yes, now she could see it. A black gun. Without any glint, mostly hidden by his loose baggy sleeve, but he let them see it.

She looked at Mike.

"We'd better do it," he said.

"Don't talk," said the man. "Move! Keep moving! Get in the alley."

There was no one else anywhere in sight.

They turned into the alley. The paving was uneven and broken in places with missing bricks. She had to look down to watch her step.

"Keep moving," said the man. "Don't stop."

She had carried nothing but her keys so she kept her hands in her pockets. The man didn't tell her not to; he only wanted her to move, move. None of this actually concerned her at all; she was not really involved. Mike had the money. It was between the two of them. She felt irritated to be dragged in on it. She did not want Mike to be hurt; neither of them could be hurt. He wasn't really going to kill them but he could. She didn't want to have to think about it.

"Move!" he said. "Move! I said move. Don't stop. Keep moving."

Mike had stopped. "I can't get at my wallet while I'm walking," he said.

The man had them stand over under a street light that brightened the alley. He wore no mask or made any attempt to hide his face. When he lifted his head, she could see all of his features very plainly.

She stood away at a slight distance.

Mike handed him the umbrella to hold while he reached inside his coat for the wallet.

The man held the umbrella out over the space between them. Neither of them was covered, just the space of the alley between them. "Hurry up," he said.

All of this did not really concern her. She stared at his face, trying to remember the detail. It was an ugly face, ugly and childish. She wished her hand in her pocket were a gun. It would make a hole right through the material in her coat. She would not ask him anything. She would not speak to him at all. She stood away at a distance and waited for Mike to pay him.

Mike counted out seven dollars. "That's all I have," he said. "No, wait a minute." He dug his hand into his pocket and brought up change. He picked his rubbing stone out and handed the rest to the man. "Will this be enough? It's all I have."

The man returned the umbrella.

Now, she thought. It's now.

"Don't talk," he said. "Just move. Start moving." He nodded along the alley.

They began walking again. She could not walk next to Mike under the umbrella. She walked along at a slight distance with her fists balled up in her pockets, carefully watching her step. Once she looked behind at the man.

"Don't turn around," he said, "or I'll blow your brains out." He was falling behind.

Now, she thought. It's right now. She tried to remember what they had been talking about before. It would let the man know how little concerned she was. He could not touch her. There was a slight irregular movement; when she turned to look, the man was vaulting over a low wooden fence.

Mike said, "Turn around."

"He's gone."

Mike looked too.

"Can you believe that?" he said.

They walked the rest of the alley; it came out very close to the place they had originally started.

Mike said, "I never want to see him again."

"I can't even remember his face," she said.

"I'll never forget his face. But I never want to see it again."

Somewhere along the way the rain had finally stopped.

Halfway down the block was the restaurant. Some people were waiting at the door for a couple to come out. The police car drove by again.

She said, "Let's get a cup of coffee."

"We don't have any money left. I gave him all the change."

The people who were waiting finally got to go inside.

She said, "Where did he come from?"

Mike went over and stood beside the car. He lowered the umbrella. "Probably hiding between the cars," he said. He started to open the door.

"Not yet," she said. "I want to go around again."

He said, "Get in."

She looked past him. "No. I'm going around."

She started walking. Mike caught up with her. "That's crazy," he said.

"You don't have to come."

He said, "The scene of the crime?"

"I want to see if he's still there."

"The whole idea is crazy," he said again. She was walking fast. But he kept up with her. "He won't be there now."

"He might. That was a stupid trick. He made us stand under the light. We could have identified him."

"You said you couldn't remember his face."

"He doesn't know that," she said. "I want to find out if he's stupid enough to try it again. He might still be waiting for his next victim."

Mike said, "And what if he is?"

"If he pops out again, we can say, 'Sorry, but we already gave.' Or 'We're broke now. You already got us first time around.' "

She started to laugh. Mike laughed too.

She poked him. "Better put the umbrella back up," she said. "We don't want any confusion."

"What do you expect to happen?"

"This time," she said. "This time we'll see."

"I hope he's not there."

"I hope he is," she said.

They passed the place where she'd first noticed the man, where he'd come out, and the place he'd stopped them. They looked down the alley.

There was no one there at all.

They walked the length of the alley again in silence.

"That's too bad," she said as they reached the car. "I hoped he'd be there."

Mike held open the door. "We could go around again," he said.

"No. The agreement was for once around the block."

He dropped her off in front of her apartment. The child was still sound asleep. There was a late movie on the television. She pulled a thick towel out of the closet and began drying her hair.

Unlike the stories by Maupassant and Chekhov, this one doesn't step right up and announce its main character. Some work is needed to puzzle that out. But attentive readers will find plenty of clues to help them. The opening miniscene introduces us to two characters, one of whom is tending a child. Whoever it is should be the point-of-view character, since the phone call is being shown as happening at that person's residence.

A few sentences into the next scene we are told, "She tried to recall a film she'd been to . . ." and the story seems immediately to tilt in her direction. The fact that the man is given a name and she is not also puts her more in the center of things. Looking at events from her perspective, then, what is the situation that gets established by the exposition and when is its business concluded?

She and Mike are involved in some sort of illicit relationship. The story leaves its terms vague, but she asks him over the phone if he will have any trouble, and when they get together she says, "You're not supposed to be seen with me." Mike seems ready to throw caution to the wind: "Oh who cares. I don't care any more." Laughing, she goes along with him: "Let 'em see. Nobody knows where we are." Yet she shrugs him off when he tries to put his arm around her. This seems to prompt his question, "Why did you come?" which leads to his assertion, "You could have said no." Clearly he considers his invitation to walk in the rain a "reasonable request," but to her it was not an invitation she could refuse. He insists, "Anyone can say no," which she counters by saying she's there now.

This disagreement fuels another one about whether it's important to make sense of everything. "She did not want to tell him how he was acting." Her disgust finally shows itself: "What a subject! What a place for a subject." This leads to a quibble about the need to walk in the rain, which ends only because she spots a man following them. End of phase one. What has "happened" so far?

For one thing, the relationship between Mike and our point-of-view character is an uneasy one. They spend most of their time bickering over seemingly petty issues. Mike is assertive, but seems defensive as well. "She" is submissive, but also evasive. The exposition also reveals some interesting ironies. We're told, "There was no reason for the walk." Yet it was Mike's "reasonable" idea, and it's Mike who insists on making sense of everything. Again, Mike says he doesn't care if he is seen with her, yet they go for a walk where they "might be invisible." Walking around in the rain "was something to do in a film but not in real life. In real life it made people plunge and curse. But not the two of them, not tonight." When he asks why she came and is told, "because you asked me to," he's unsatisfied. He wants her to have said, "because of you."

We can't claim to have learned a lot about them so far, but we must believe that the exposition has given us as much as we need to know to understand the crisis. Unlike the Maupassant or Chekhov stories, which provided information about the characters to tell readers about their background, this one jumps straight into an unfolding action and expects us to piece a context together from what we can pick up along the way.

The crisis phase is fairly clearly marked out by the coming and going of the robber. But it is less clear exactly what the nature of the crisis is. Of course there is the obvious danger—getting their brains blown out. But this threat is handled in a way to play down its significance. Our main character doesn't even seem to feel that she is involved in the holdup: "All of this did not really concern her. . . . She stood away at a distance and waited for Mike to pay him."

So then, if it's not a question of possible physical violence, what is the episode's significance? How is the main character's status quo disturbed? In what way is she deflected? The robber says to get in the alley, to move and not to talk, to hurry up with the money. He is making requests. Are they "reasonable" in the same sense as Mike's request that she go walking with him? Can Mike say no to them? If not, do they disprove Mike's contention that "anyone can say no"? Does the holdup pose a question that can be answered? Is there something about it to make sense of? If not, is Mike's claim that everyone feels a personal responsibility to find the rational answer also invalidated? Finally, if Mike is somehow repudiated by the assault, how does that change our main character's thinking? What is the meaning of her thought, "Now. It's right now"?

Keeping in mind that this is a modern story with a deliberately ambiguous "message," we can still be pretty certain of some things. For instance, it's clear that whatever has happened, she becomes much less submissive, much more assertive in the final scene, just as Mike seems to lose aggressiveness and turn fairly docile. It is possible to see the attack in the alley as a metaphoric sexual encounter. "Mike erected the umbrella and opened her door. She came up under his umbrella." *Erected* is an unusual word to use in this context unless intended to suggest something sexual. The umbrella is a convenient phallic symbol. His opening her door and her coming up under his umbrella take on an obvious meaning.

Reading the scene in the alley as a sexual encounter explains some of the woman's reactions. The robber, doubling for Mike, points a gun and threatens to shoot, but she feels nothing. While the robber holds his umbrella, Mike pays him everything he has. Once Mike is "spent," the robber departs. She feels unconcerned. "He could not touch her."

Looked at so, we sense that Mike forces himself on her, demanding her compliance, wanting her affection but unable to compel that. Hence, she is unaffected. When she decides to "go around again," she is giving the robber another chance to show himself. She wants to find out "if he's stupid enough to try it again." She is now in charge, looking for answers, trying to make sense of things, he the timid follower who calls the whole idea crazy. The roles have been reversed. Whether we read the story as a metaphoric sexual episode or a literal holdup, the significance is similar: the incident in the alley shows her something about Mike, or men, or both, that somehow makes her strong and free. It isn't as straightforward as a Maupassant tale, but it's just as structured, every bit as much a story.

You should now be ready to do a structural analysis all on your own. You can pick any story you please, but it's especially satisfying to examine some story that intrigued you when you read it but didn't make much sense to you at the time. Whatever story you choose, make a photocopy of it (so you can mark it up) and dig in. Can you break it into three phases? Can you find a main character? Does he/she meet with a significant crisis? What sort of changes does that crisis bring? How is the main character "deflected"? What seems to be the "message" of the overall story?

The more stories you analyze in this way, the better your sense of story structure will become. You'll learn something new about technique from every story you read. You'll come to appreciate more fully how many ways there are to put stories together. Not every story will fall neatly into the three-phase pattern: exposition may be mingled in with the developing crisis; phase three is sometimes cut short, leaving the consequences implied; there may be two main characters, each competing for prominence and somehow both participating equally in the crisis.

Ideally, you should spend considerable time studying short fiction in this way. But you are likely to be anxious to move on to writing your own story. So once you're confident you can spot a main character and a deflection and identify the three phases, you should be ready for Chapter 2, and your first writing assignment.

• two •

RECOLLECTION

THE BASIC STUFF OF FICTION—REAL LIFE

You've done your warm-ups and are ready to begin writing in earnest. You're sure you know what a short story looks like well enough to start building one of your own. But *The Primer* still hasn't told you how to dream up that opening scene or even crank out your opening sentence. If you're eager to write, that's good. You'll have plenty of writing to do soon. But don't expect to "dream up" anything straight off or even produce an opening sentence. Both of those will have to wait a little. Meanwhile, you still have a few more pages to read before you get to that first writing assignment. Don't be tempted to jump the gun and skip ahead. It will just mean backtracking later on.

But what's this about not getting to make things up? Isn't that what fiction's all about—inventing characters and then imagining lives for them to live? Yes, but inventing and imagining need something to draw on, like a flower sending out a bloom. A plant's roots reach into the soil to find the food it needs to produce flowers. The visible beauty of the flower is made possible by the work of the roots. Fiction requires imagination, but imagination needs roots in real life to sustain it.

Probably the worst mistake beginning fiction writers can make is to ignore their own lives as starting points for stories. Young persons seem especially ready to devalue the worth of their own experience. Their reasoning seems to go something like this: Nothing exciting ever happens to me, so if I tell about my life it's bound to bore the socks off my readers, who are only reading my story in the hope of escaping from their own boring lives.

There is a grain of truth embedded in this circular reasoning. We may as well admit it right off: those who read strictly for escape won't be content with ordinary reality. The kind of story *The Primer* helps you write is definitely "reality based," so the story you're going to write won't satisfy the escapist's needs. But there are at least two good reasons for not being upset about that. First, once you've done a *Primer* basic story, you'll be prepared to start writing escape stories if you want (see chapter 11). Second, and more important, most fiction readers are not looking for escape anyhow. What they really want is to get into other people's lives, to feel what those other people are experiencing and try to understand and sympathize with their problems.

The average fiction reader's needs are not fancy. Most don't want godlike heroes or weird goings on or strange settings. They want familiar scenes with real-seeming people doing understandable things for common-sense reasons. That's why soap operas are so popular. For all their bad plotting and weak characterizations they do try to show "average" people coping with everyday difficulties in normal human ways, so that ordinary viewers can share the experience. Instead of escaping from reality, they explore and exploit it. Your story won't have many soap opera qualities, but it will tap into the same source of power it uses—real life.

THE BEST MATERIAL AVAILABLE

You may still be concerned that the only real life you know is your own, and no matter how you cut it it's still too boring to be good fiction. Or put another way, a story's supposed to be about an *important* event in some imagined person's life, and you're not imaginary and nothing important has ever happened to you. How are you supposed to get around that? First, quit thinking of your own life as boring. Henry David Thoreau's life at Walden Pond was as unexciting as a life could be, but his account of it makes fascinating reading. Why? Because Thoreau observed things closely, felt them keenly, and wrote about them precisely.

If Thoreau had found his life tiresome or trivial, his writing would have been equally unexciting. Plenty of jet-setters are bored with their "thrilling" lives because in spite of all the movement, nothing much seems to happen to them. Action alone won't keep readers interested; they've got to be *involved.* Documentary animal-life films prove that almost any activity can be intriguing watched through a zoom lens. The point is, if you can make your story seem *important* to your readers, it will engage their attention almost regardless of what it's about. Equally, no matter how action-packed, if your story doesn't draw readers into its world and make them care about the problems of its characters, they'll find it dull and tiresome in a hurry.

The trick, then, isn't blowing readers out of their seats, it's keeping them glued there with a hypnotic stream of fascinating details. You make things visible by describing what's there to be seen. You also note the sounds, smells, tastes, and textures that will enable readers to share your world. You make sure to include essential non-sensory data like thoughts and feelings. Only after you've succeeded in putting readers "in the picture" can you hope to interest them in what your characters are up to.

Beginning writers sometimes get the cart before the horse by first concocting a weird plotline and only then start hoping that some believable characters will happen along to make it come to life. Better start with a bit of experience that feels real and use it as a foundation to build your story on. It's the surest way of avoiding unbelievable castles in the air.

The source of this "experience that feels real"? Where else but your own back yard. The life you know at first hand is the life you can report at first hand. You know no other experience half so well, and no one else knows your experience half so well as you do. It's one subject you can truly claim to be the world's leading authority on. Because you're so familiar with it, you can draw from it with total assurance that the details are accurate. And because you understand your own hopes and motives better than anyone else, you can speak of them with energy and directness.

But what if, after all the arguments in favor of using personal experience as your story's starting point, you're still not happy with the idea? What if you simply can't bear the thought of basing anything on any part of your own life, or just can't find a single piece of it that seems interesting enough to use? The short answer to that question is, Fake it. In other words, if you really can't locate the necessary starter material in your actual experience (and I do mean "can't locate" rather than "don't have"), you will need to begin the process of invention now rather than later, and *imagine* an incident that you can *pretend* happened to you. Since the main purpose for using a real-life starter is to insure that you write about what you know about, as long as you can honestly say that the incident you use *could have happened* to you, that main purpose will have been served. Since you're not an alien, you won't be writing about life on some other planet—not in this first story. Unless you're a cowboy, no "westerns." And no historical romance, since you couldn't have been there to see it happen. It has to be either your life or a reasonable facsimile thereof. And whether you begin with the "real" reality of your actual life or with an invented reality that you might have lived, once you're past this first writing assignment you'll be making it up anyway.

PICKING THE RIPE FRUIT

You may already have mulled over some of your life's more crucial events that might serve as "starter" material. Or you may still be convinced that your life doesn't contain any starters. At this point you're probably better off not knowing where to begin. That way you'll make your search with a completely open mind. Amid all the experiences of your life, how do you select the one to base your first story on? First of all, remember the importance of deflection. A story is a "turning point" experience. So you'll need to retrace your life looking for those days when things happened to deflect you from your normal straight-line progress and change your attitude to life in a fundamental way.

If your mind works like most people's, the experiences that tend to rush forward are the big, dramatic ones—a harrowing car wreck or skiing accident or your near death from mononucleosis. But even though such material might guarantee strong scenes, it doesn't always contain any significant deflection.

Suppose, for instance, that from early childhood you'd set your heart on being a circus aerialist and spent years practicing high-wire and trapeze routines, but an ugly fall from a motel balcony left you permanently crippled. Obviously a turning point (right?) since it forced a drastic alteration in your future plans. But the question is, did your change in attitude occur *during the time period to be covered*? Chances are, you didn't immediately decide that your aerialist career was out of reach for good. You probably avoided thinking much about that possibility—it would have been too painful.

So the actual change in your outlook most likely began later on, after the doctors began hinting that your disability was going to be permanent. Which means that a story about your accident wouldn't use the fall itself as the crisis, because the deflection in your understanding didn't occur till some time later. Making the fall be the story's crisis would distort the situation's psychological values and so damage its credibility.

Hear and heed some lofty-sounding words of advice from the British novelist, Victoria Sackville-West: "Physical incidents are seldom worth dwelling on in fiction, however disagreeably large they may bulk in life; the sagacious novelist hurries on to the psychological situation thus adventitiously produced, skipping any explanation of an event which is indeed, by reasonable processes, inexplicable."

Another helpful question to ask yourself about a possible crisis episode is, Did I have to consider options and make a choice? Looked at this way, that fall from a motel balcony seems to lack "deliberation." About all you'd have time for is to brace for the impact. You certainly wouldn't be pondering your options or making conscious choices. Think of the stories by Maupassant, Chekhov, and Doud. When Lantin learns that his dead wife's jewels are worth a fortune, he has to face up to what that implies about her supposed purity before he can consider whether he will profit from the discovery. Mashenka must come to terms with her anger and shame before she can decide how to respond to Madame Kushkin's insults. The main character in "The Reasonable Request" is changed by the holdup, not because the thief steals anything material from her, but because the experience causes her to see things differently.

Robert Frost wrote: "Two roads diverged, and I—I took the one less traveled by, /And that has made all the difference." Stories always happen at the crossroads where a person has to go one way rather than another. Of course not every story tells of a choice that made "all the difference," but your main character's turning point must be important enough to take a reader's interest along with it.

One sure way to forfeit most readers' interest in a hurry is to ask them to believe what their common sense tells them is not believable. One of the perversities of human nature is that we like to hear of "amazing" things happening in real life (e.g., Ripley's "Believe it or not?" or TV's "That's Incredible!"), but we don't want "real life" in a piece of fiction to seem at all implausible. What this means for you is, don't choose a crisis incident that seemed remarkable even though it happened to you. In general, avoid any event that has a supercharged, "operatic" quality about it—chances are, if it already feels heightened, it will get hyped into melodrama by being fictionalized.

JUST THREE MORE THINGS TO KEEP IN MIND

1. Be sure the turning point incident you choose to start with really is a single event, not a loose cluster of actions or a string of thoughts. You must be able to pin it down to a specific time—the more specific the better. Usually, an episode of human confrontation will play out in under an hour. If the scene you plan to summarize goes on much longer than that, you may not be narrowing it down sufficiently. In this regard, be guided more by the Chekhov and Doud stories than by the Maupassant. Of course some crises really do last a whole day or more (as Maupassant's "The Jewels" illustrates), but you should aim for closer to ten minutes, real time. And don't

worry that your account will feel incomplete. Lacking its "before" and "after" phases, it's bound to. You'll deal with that deficiency later on.

2. Keep the scale of your central issue "personal" rather than "global." If you make your characters debate large, controversial questions, their personalities will end up playing second fiddle to the big ideas and you'll end up with a piece of propaganda rather than a short story. A mother and daughter arguing about birth control or a father and son disagreeing on capital punishment will almost certainly yield poor fiction. The characters will be mouthpieces for "sides" and lose their individual identity. Mashenka doesn't discuss "human dignity" or "individual rights" with anyone. She is too caught up in her own particular predicament to be thinking in grand terms. She has been attacked, and her concern is to protect her self-esteem. At this point she isn't worried about winning or losing arguments, but about defending her personal values.
3. Finally, a special requirement made necessary by *The Primer*'s unique procedure: the experience must have been shared by another person who also would have felt its impact strongly. The sharer can be a friendly rival or actual enemy, a fellow sufferer or a collaborator, anyone who played a part and had a real stake in what happened. But, you ask, how can you be sure just how much somebody else is affected by anything? All right, then, let this be your first creative act. Let your imagination speculate about this other person's reactions. Since he or she was right there with you, you have some actual words and actions to guide you in figuring out thoughts and motives. Don't bother at this point to work up a complete analysis of this other person. It's enough for now to be sure that the sharer of your experience was also deflected by it.

TO WRITE AT LAST?

Well, almost. You've got a shopping list of guidelines to check against core samples from your life:

1. turning point or deflection
2. choice of options
3. no operatic melodrama
4. single short scene
5. specific issue
6. shared experience.

If you're at all vague about any of these requisites, you ought to go back and read the sections about them over again before continuing. If you're confident you understand your checklist, it's time to try some sifting.

Let's suppose a few minutes' brainstorming has picked out the following possible starter kernels:

> Your visit to Grandfather in the hospital when he told you he was dying.
>
> Attending a high school reunion and learning how much difference twenty years can make.
>
> Returning to its owner a wallet with fifty dollars in it which you found in a parking lot.
>
> Your second-place finish in the regional tennis tournament.

They all look promising enough as possible turning points in your own life, but will they measure up to each of the five requirements on your list? The scene with Grandfather could be risky for several reasons. First, it's likely to go mushy with sentiment or shrill with melodrama, or both. Second, how much real change occurs? Your feeling for him may seem stronger than ever, but it's probably the same feeling you've had for him all along. Third, what about *his* feelings? It's even less likely to be a turning point for him. After all, he has probably known he was dying for some time, so that telling you doesn't change things for him. Finally, the farther you are from being as old now as your grandfather was then, the harder it would be to see and feel things from his vantage point. (Writing about ten-year-olds when you're sixty can also be difficult, if you've forgotten what being ten is like.)

As for the reunion, it probably covers too long a period of time. If you tried to recount the entire experience, or even most of it, that could get pretty tedious. You need to narrow the timeframe to a specific few minutes when you and some *one* of your former chums shared a turning-point experience that left you both permanently changed, for better or worse.

Finding and returning a wallet suggests two scenes rather than just one. And who is the sharer of the incident—the wallet's owner, or someone with you when you found it? And how were you—and that other person—changed by the experience?

Coming in second in a big competition can certainly be a turning-point experience, as the sample student narrative (below) will show. But sports narratives often become childish fables in which generic foes struggle to prove tired morals—"Victory to the righteous," or "Chance favors the bold," or "It's not whether you win or lose but how you play the game." Remember, you must never let your theme turn your characters into cardboard spokesmen.

As these samples suggest, even when you hit on good material you can easily miss the bull's-eye. Don't hesitate to move backward or forward along the timeline to find the best deflection point to use for your starter incident. Grandfather's speech in the hospital may be what you first remember, but the quiet afternoon you played checkers together when he didn't say anything "profound" may have been more of a turning point for both of you. Coming second in that tennis tournament may have seemed a great achievement (or disaster), yet may have had less real impact on your outlook than the encounter you had with the winner in the locker room after it was all over. Finding the true center of a story idea can be like focusing a camera lens or tuning in a radio station—crossing and recrossing the right spot will make it stand out clear against the background blur.

Once you've settled on your starter incident, you're ready to write—at last.

Your First Writing Assignment

Here's what you do: Summarize, in no more than 300-400 words, the essential details of the experience you have selected. Tell it in first person (that is, from the standpoint of a narrator called "I"), in standard, mid-level English prose (that is, neither too slangy nor too fancy) and in strict chronological sequence (that is, exactly in the order it happened in real time). You will not have space to include many particulars, but you should be able to make your overall account of what occurred and how you felt about it clear enough for readers to follow what went on in both the exterior world of action and the internal one of perception.

Don't be deceived by this assignment's shortness or seeming simplicity into taking it casually. It is a modest but vital first step, one that will lay the foundation and set the course of the entire story to follow. You will have to live with whatever plan you make now, for better or worse, the rest of the way. So this is a time for careful consideration and "deliberate" writing.

When you have finished, read the following transcript of one student's response to this assignment (hereafter called Narrative A). It is provided not as a model to be imitated, but as a sample of a satisfactory starter incident.

Sample Narrative A

The girls' chorus quit singing "Somewhere My Love" when the familiar crackling from the wooden box on the wall told us an announcement was about to be made. As the soprano section buzzed with "shush" and "be quiet," I felt the sweat behind my knees. Mr. Smith's voice exhaled loudly, then asked for our attention. He was going to tell us the winners of the student council elections.

My toes clung to the soles of my sandals at the mention of Julia Adams. With Kathy Bonner, my shoulders began tightening. Bobby Carson had me clenching my hands. Then it was out—my own name! And I finally breathed again. There was no mistake. Loud and clear, I'd made it.

When I finally remembered to listen for Kim's name, the announcement was ended and the entire chorus was in a stir. I looked over at Kim sitting open-mouthed, staring blankly at the intercom, and I knew her name hadn't been one of the ones announced.

Girls were patting me on the back, congratulating me and telling me they knew I'd make it as I went over to where Kim sat. I put my hand on her shoulder, but couldn't think of a thing to say. She shook my hand off and turned away from me. She put her hands over her eyes and I knew she was crying.

A friend of mine came over and told me how great it was I'd been elected, and I felt like killing her. All I could think of was how to comfort Kim. Till then I hadn't realized how much I'd been looking forward to being in student council because Kim would be there too.

Then she stood up, walked to the table where she'd left her geometry book and purse, and picked them up as if they didn't matter at all to her any more. I tagged after her, still not knowing what to do or say. Finally she said she guessed it didn't make all that much difference. What did a stupid school election matter anyhow?

And I said, "You're right, Kim, it's nothing but a popularity contest." As soon as the words were out of my mouth I could have bit my tongue. She gave me a look I'll never forget, turned, and walked away.

This summarized incident meets all the requirements of the writing assignment quite well. It is narrated straightforwardly in ordinary prose, in first person, and in strict chronological order. We can follow the exterior series of events and also our first-person narrator's reactions to those events as they occur. The account focuses on two persons, and both seem to have been strongly affected by the experience. Kim is a classmate of the narrator, so they're about the same age, and good friends, so the author should have a pretty clear understanding of Kim's personality. Also, the incident feels like the middle of a story, lacking—and needing—both a "set-up" to prepare us for it and a "follow-up" to take us on through to some resolution. Most important, it gives readers a believable bit of human experience to get interested in, a pair of fellow humans to sympathize with. It has, then, what Henry James called "felt life"—the essential heartbeat of any story.

• three •

SPECULATION

WHY REAL LIFE ISN'T ENOUGH

After all the talk in chapter 2 about how important "life" is to fiction and a first writing assignment that's mainly a memory exercise, you may be wondering when the creativity starts. The answer is, everything so far including that memory exercise *was* part of the creative process. A potter doesn't start shaping clay on a wheel until he has both clay and a wheel *and* some awareness of what it is he's trying to make and an understanding of the technique needed to turn spinning clay lumps into artworks. Chapter 1 gave you an appreciation of just what stories are, how they are put together. In chapter 2 you "dug out" a starting lump of clay. With that much accomplished you're ready to take on the more obviously creative job of spinning the clay into a pot.

Of course you've known all along that the time would come when your fancy had to take off and fly. Chances are, you've been looking forward to this liftoff with some eagerness. In case you're actually feeling some dread, be assured you won't be asked to fly all at once. Like everything else in *The Primer*, your progress will happen so gradually that you'll hardly feel your feet leave the ground. But whether making things up seems appealing or appalling, you may be wondering why it's necessary to do anything to real life to turn it into fiction. If life's the ultimate basic stuff, why tamper with it at all? Wouldn't using it "straight" make the strongest fiction possible?

In the first place, life is life and writing is writing and the twain can never meet. Writing about life doesn't make life out of words. Lived life is straight experience. Life in print, no matter how accurately presented, is still presented. You experience it second hand, vicariously. Even if you wanted to put life on a sheet of paper, you couldn't do it. You couldn't even come close. There are just too many data bits in every speck of life for a complete report to be possible. You'd need at least the rest of your life just to note them down and as long again to read them, which would be not only a waste of time but a misrepresentation of how that one poor speck passed. So when we tell what happened to us yesterday, we don't really bring back the past. We pick out a few details from the infinite number there were and expect our listener/reader to fill in the rest well enough to make sense of our narrative.

The biggest difference between fiction and "real life" accounts is the way their details get selected. The details of a personal experience narrative are normally chosen at random from the narrator's memory. Think of the way you retell an experience: A backward glance across the whole event's timespan to remind yourself of its broad outline and main points, then a quick walk-through from start to finish noting only the most conspicuous developments. You take what your memory offers you, trusting it to provide the most important data. But if you've ever had to explain "what happened" to a policeman or a lawyer, you know just how inadequate your memory can be in judging the significance of data. What may have seemed too obvious or too trivial to be worth recalling can turn out to be vital evidence.

So then, instead of changing anything, wouldn't it be best just to probe our memories thoroughly, as if we were policemen or lawyers after "the truth," until we've set down a "full confession"? That way we wouldn't end up with random recall. The record would be thorough, balanced, and above all, factual. After all, isn't that what historical fiction writers try to do, to give us as accurate a picture of past events as they can, as close to what a sound camera would have filmed as they can? In a word, no. Historical fiction simply uses the names of persons alleged (by other writers!) to have lived on planet Earth in past time and participated in events that got above-average publicity.

It's only fair to point out that historical fiction writers don't claim to be making genuine reconstructions of the events they use in their stories. Mary Renault's characterization of Theseus or Alexander is at best conjecture. The hard evidence for what they really did is sketchy and fragmentary. Their personal qualities could be known only to their contemporary associates. Gore Vidal has chosen to depict figures like the Emperor Julian and Aaron Burr more favorably than most accounts show them in an effort to set the record straight. Since history gets written by the winners, Vidal believes "establishment" record keepers can't help distorting the motives and achievements of "enemies of the State" in the interest of "national security." Of course his slant, too, is no more than an educated guess, but he says his "truth" is better researched and documented than the "facts" our history texts have been passing along to unsuspecting generations of students.

This doesn't mean that most historians are grossly dishonest or wickedly inexact, only that both they and the fiction writers who base stories on historical accounts have only an imperfect knowledge of "the facts." Really to know what happened, even if you saw it in person, is impossible. Ten witnesses to anything will give ten different accounts of it afterward, for at least two reasons: first, no one vantage point is the same as any other, so that no one viewer sees exactly what anyone else does; second, no matter how hard anybody tries to be strictly objective, nobody ever can be. This being so, it could be said that all writing is some kind of fiction, either conscious (intentional) or unconscious (accidental). Since your only choice is between knowing and not knowing you're "telling a story," you are better able to control what your story means if you tell it knowing it is fiction.

Once you realize that you can't help imposing your attitudes on whatever you write, you'll see why real life, as is, won't work as fiction. Life is a haphazard and miscellaneous string of happenings that doesn't seem to move forward with much consistency or efficiency. No matter how hard we look, life doesn't seem to have much shape, either while being lived or when looked back on afterward. If there is some pattern of thematic meaning, some "grand design" in our individual lives, it is far too complex for most of us to see. Without sorting, life is an utter tangle of events.

In order to show life making sense, we really have to adapt it, interpret it, make it up. Life may not have a theme, but a story will, because its author has to have a basis for deciding what details belong and what do not. That basis for sorting relevant from irrelevant data *is* theme. Chekhov's "Turmoil" may seem on first reading to lack the tight structure and careful data selection of Maupassant's "The Jewels." It feels less made up, more like real life, but it is actually just as contrived, just as managed. The only difference is that Chekhov camouflaged his design more carefully so as to make it easier for a reader to share the experience. As you learned back in chapter 1, every detail in a well-crafted short story contributes to a single central purpose and so supports the thematic unity of the whole.

WHAT THE READER EXPECTS

Fortunately, having to make your stories up doesn't make you a liar in your readers' eyes. Fiction readers don't expect or *want* "facts." They may not be able to tell you why, exactly, but they understand perfectly well that fiction is a fabrication, made up in a writer's head, not a report of events that really happened. They know that reporting is a journalist's work, not a fiction writer's. They expect you to understand this too, and to show you do by how you handle your story. Meaning that they want you to take full responsibility for what occurs, so they can feel sure that all is happening according to plan. Tell fiction readers you're going to give them a "true story" and they'll know you're kidding. If you're not kidding, you're not writing fiction.

Fiction is an adult version of "Let's Pretend" played between a writer and a reader, an ancient cooperative game with certain understood rules that have to be accepted by both participants. The writer has the privilege of guiding the reader through a series of imaginary events that he claims will interest the reader, if the reader will only pay attention. The reader meantime enjoys the privilege of taking the guided tour, possibly even learning something from it, and the duty to accept the writer's illusion of reality as gospel for the duration of the story. Coleridge called this act of reader faith "a willing suspension of disbelief." In a way it's like submitting to hypnosis—you have to let the hypnotist cast his spell in order to see with the clarity of hypnotic vision.

Are readers really so unsuspecting, so willing to be duped, that they're ready to accept without question any cock-and-bull story you want to tell them? Well no, not quite. If you don't give them a good enough picture to look at, you can't expect them to take it seriously. Their attention will flag, their belief fail. But what's important is that they will *try* to believe. The instinct of a fiction reader favors the case the storyteller is trying to put. That's why it's a "willing" suspension of disbelief. An angler's paradise: the fish actually *want* to be hooked.

If readers didn't want to believe, fiction simply couldn't happen. You wouldn't think it could work: an invisible stranger offers to give you a blow-by-blow account of some event, complete with a detailed description of its setting and the people involved, including their every noteworthy speech, move, gesture, expression and, best of all, running commentary on their thoughts and feelings throughout? Would you trust anyone making such wild claims? If he's a fiction writer and you're a fiction reader, the answer is, "Sure, why not?" If you don't think so, if that's not the way you *read* a work of fiction, you'll need to adjust your thinking about *writing* it.

THE FICTION CONTRACT

The reason why "real life" won't work as fiction, then, is simply that fiction expects more from a narrative than mere documentary accuracy. Factual accounts, such as newspaper reporting of actual occurrences, are primarily concerned with making a clear summary of a series of events. Their intent is *to explain*. Their approach is therefore "expository." Fictional accounts, on the other hand, are primarily concerned with revealing the *meaning* of a series of events. Because their intent is to interpret, their approach is "persuasive." Thus, factual writing and fictional writing differ at the most basic level of purpose and so are guided by very different assumptions and attitudes.

For a piece of fiction to work, both writer and reader have to abide by a contract that reads something like this:

> Everything that happens in this story does so by permission of its author in accordance with some plan and purpose that will be complete and intelligible by the time all its events have been told.

When fiction writers narrate developments in their characters' lives, they can be certain their readers will know such events are fabricated without being told, even if the events are made to appear as life-like as possible. Because there is no way for the reader to test whether the story is actually made up or not, both writer and reader have to depend on their mutually honoring the fiction contract and sharing fiction's *attitude*.

This puts a special burden on writers to live up to their readers' faith in them. Story readers have to trust that an author is playing by the rules, whereas the author knows whether he is or not. To cheat someone in such circumstances would be as shabby as it would be easy. Consequently, fiction writers are pledged, as part of their code of good practice, *not* to "tell the truth." To stick to facts would be to defraud story readers, who expect to be given a hypothesis to speculate about. Imagine telling a story in completely objective language and from a totally neutral perspective; imagine it meandering along just like life with no theme or focus developing, and with characters moving haphazardly, the way people really do. It wouldn't make any difference that you'd made such a story up. Readers would look in vain for clues to what you meant in your story, and wouldn't find any—clues or meaning. You would have betrayed their trust.

Your Second Writing Assignment

Now that you know why the "unvarnished truth" of real life won't work as fiction, you are ready for your next writing assignment. From now on, you must accept that the sense of your story depends on yourself, not on that "reality" you're drawing it from. Beginning writers often confuse authenticity with plausibility. A Vietnam veteran introduces a mound of decomposing corpses into his story, and when readers object that it doesn't mean anything he argues, "But that's the way it was," as if that mattered. What counts is whether it *seems* real. Fiction is about experience, to be sure, but it's not about "what really happened." No amount of "raw" reality can make up for a lack of plausibility, no matter how high you stack it.

In Narrative A, you wrote a first-person ("I" narrator) account of a turning-point experience in your life. If you picked that experience according to instructions, you shared it with someone else for whom it was also important. Your second writing assignment will be to write another 300-400 word, first-person account of the same scene, but this time *from the position of that other person*. In other words, you will pretend to be that other person and use his or her manner and voice to relate the identical events you told from your own standpoint in Narrative A.

But before turning your writing hand loose on this new project, take some time to think about the individual qualities of this other being you're going to impersonate. The person is probably someone you're well acquainted with, perhaps a close friend or relation you feel you've known "all your life," whose personality is as familiar as home.

But remember, no matter how near or dear other persons may be to you, your view of them has always been from the outside. You've never tried living in another human's skin before, seeing and feeling things the way they would, rather than the way you do.

The question to ask yourself is, Will I be able to take on this other identity so totally I can actually see the world, myself included, through those alien eyes? It isn't necessary to convince yourself another person's view of things is superior to your own. But when you assume that other role, you must also be able to adopt all its inner qualities, stand by its principles, take up and defend its causes. Hardest of all, you should be able to do a convincing job of expanding or contracting your own understanding to the size of this other mind.

As a first step to firming up and fleshing out your understanding of this other personality, use the following checklist of characteristics to define a "personality profile" for him or her. Put X's beside all words that describe the person, XX's or even XXX's beside especially strong indicators. Just as important, mark all words that seem *opposite* to the person's actual qualities with O's (or OO's or even OOO's), so that you have two sets of "index attributes," one positive and one negative. You should have little difficulty tagging this list of characteristics if you really do have a clear sense of the person's character. If your responses are slow, doubtful, or tentative, you probably need a surer grasp of this personality you intend to assume. Just working through the checklist ought to help you discover much you can use.

Checklist of Personal Characteristics

____ academic
____ accurate
____ adaptable
____ adventurous
____ affected
____ affectionate
____ aggressive
____ alert
____ ambitious
____ argumentative
____ arrogant
____ articulate
____ artistic
____ attractive
____ biased
____ bitter
____ boisterous
____ broadminded
____ businesslike
____ callous
____ calm
____ capable
____ careful
____ careless
____ cautious
____ charming
____ cheerful
____ clear-thinking
____ clever
____ cold
____ competent
____ competitive
____ confident
____ conscientious
____ conservative
____ considerate
____ cool
____ cooperative
____ courageous
____ cowardly
____ cruel
____ crusty
____ curious
____ daring
____ deliberate
____ determined
____ devious
____ dignified
____ discreet
____ disloyal
____ dominant
____ eager
____ easygoing
____ efficient
____ emotional
____ energetic
____ fair-minded
____ farsighted
____ fickle
____ firm
____ flexible
____ forceful
____ frank
____ friendly
____ generous
____ gentle
____ good-natured
____ healthy
____ heartless
____ helpful
____ honest
____ hostile
____ humorous
____ idealistic
____ imaginative

____ impressionable
____ improvident
____ impulsive
____ incompetent
____ independent
____ individualistic
____ industrious
____ informal
____ insecure
____ insensitive
____ intellectual
____ intelligent
____ inventive
____ irritable
____ kind
____ lazy
____ light-hearted
____ likable
____ logical
____ loyal
____ mature
____ methodical
____ meticulous
____ mild
____ moderate
____ modest
____ morose
____ narrow-minded
____ natural
____ obliging
____ open-minded
____ opportunistic
____ optimistic
____ organized
____ original
____ outgoing
____ painstaking
____ patient
____ peaceable
____ persevering
____ pessimistic
____ placid
____ pleasant
____ poised
____ polite
____ practical
____ precise
____ progressive
____ prudent
____ purposeful
____ quick
____ quiet
____ rational
____ realistic
____ reckless
____ reflective
____ relaxed
____ reliable
____ reserved
____ resourceful
____ responsible
____ retiring
____ rigid
____ robust
____ rude
____ self-confident
____ self-controlled
____ sensible
____ sensitive
____ serious
____ sharp-witted
____ sincere
____ sly
____ sneaky
____ sociable
____ spontaneous
____ spunky
____ stable
____ steady
____ stern
____ strong
____ strong-minded
____ stubborn
____ stupid
____ subservient
____ sullen
____ surly
____ suspicious
____ sympathetic
____ tactful
____ tactless
____ teachable
____ tenacious
____ thorough
____ thoughtful
____ timid
____ tolerant
____ tough
____ trustworthy
____ unaffected
____ unassuming
____ understanding
____ unexcitable
____ uninhibited
____ versatile
____ violent
____ warm
____ wholesome
____ willful
____ wise
____ zany

Having identified the characteristics on the list that you feel are most (and least) typical of the attitudes and behavior of this person (named B), you should now see how apparent the traits you've picked out are in B's actions in your Narrative A. If you find places where B doesn't behave according to how he or she should have, according to your checklist profile, you need to be able to explain why. Motives are often kept concealed, feelings get suppressed, thoughts go unspoken. Maybe this particular bit of B's life simply didn't bring B's usual qualities clearly into play After reviewing B's words and deeds in Narrative A and squaring them with your personality profile for B, you should select a set of *no more than ten* characteristics that you feel in combination fairly well explains B's part in Narrative A.

This "working profile" set of characteristics need not be drawn only from items already on the checklist. For example, the author of our sample Narrative A came up with this profile for the character of Kim: aggressive, impulsive, individualistic, insecure, sharp-witted, suspicious, willful. Having a short list of specific attributes like this in mind will help you keep B's personality fresh and lively. At the same time, it will serve to remind you of those aspects of B's character your story is going to focus on, and so be a quick guide to what your characterization needs to emphasize.

If you begin to worry, as you make your list, about whether you are doing justice to the real, flesh-and-blood B, just remember what was said earlier—you couldn't stick to the facts about B even if you wanted to, and as a fiction writer you shouldn't want to anyway. So if you come up with a mix of ingredients that you like the look and feel of, don't fret about being "unfaithful" to the model you're drawing from. Your purpose, after all, is not to do a biographical sketch of your best friend or your great aunt, but to write an original story. Which means that your loyalty is to this invented character, "B," not the true-life person whose personality helped stir your imagination.

But what if, no matter how much you tell yourself this, you just can't escape the clutches of the true-life B, whose character refuses to let you tamper with it? Trying to walk around in such a personality would be like trying to waltz in a suit of armor—you'd never do it comfortably or gracefully. So if your model won't let you either modify or manipulate its workings, better scrap it now before it discourages you. Get yourself another true-life B, one you don't owe such respect.

Think of all the truly "wrong-headed" people you've known—insensitive teachers, obnoxious clerks, power-mad baby sitters. No feeling that they deserve to be handled with care, right? Just be sure that your hostility or contempt for the real person doesn't turn your fictional person into an implausible monster. Remember, you have to be able to understand, even to sympathize with your central character's attitudes. Ideally, what you want is someone enough like yourself that you feel in touch with his/her outlook and yet different enough from you that you never forget you're only pretending.

Once you're securely inside B's skin, reread your Narrative A. Pause over each sentence. Examine every bit of evidence it presents with a critical eye—the critical eye of B, that is. Keep reminding yourself of your differences from the writer of Narrative A and ask yourself if you can buy A's version of things. Remember, no two persons ever see the same events the same way. As B, you're sure to differ from A in your view of the events in Narrative A. So be prepared to challenge each statement with a skeptical "Oh, really?" or "Sure, *you'd* put it that way," or "Who do you think you're kidding?" or even "Rubbish!" After subjecting A's account to this sort of cross-examination, you should be able to make a convincing job of telling it over from B's standpoint.

The student author of Narrative A in chapter 2 produced the following:

Sample Narrative B

Somewhere between "a hill blossoms in green and gold" and "there are dreams" Mr. Smith's harsh tones crackling over the intercom stopped our chorus's feeble attempt at "Somewhere My Love." I'd been waiting for this moment for months, ever since Linda and I decided we'd get ourselves elected to student council. She was my campaign manager, and I was hers. So we were each working as hard as we could to get us both in.

There it was, Linda's name. She'd made it—all right! Now all I had to do was wait for my own name. Mr. Smith was bound to say "Kim." He'd never cared for me, I knew, but he didn't pick student council winners. He might not like my style, but the junior class knew me, knew I was the right one for this job.

But then why wasn't my name called? Was Mr. Smith really taking it out on me for wearing noisy shoes from Hong Kong that clattered in the halls? Who was it that counted the ballots—Mrs. O'Connell? She'd be glad to cheat me if she got the chance. All this stir around me, what's going on? Congratulations, Julie! Way to go, Linda! What about Kim? Nobody even remembers Kim was in the running. All I could think was, "I can't believe it."

Then I felt a hand on my shoulder and saw Linda out of the corner of my eye. Who are you to come and console me? I wanted to scream at her. You don't know what it is to lose, in your silly red sun dress. Everybody thinks you're just terrific, because you're just *like* everybody. Oh, get away, I don't need your gloating sympathy!

I guess I must have started crying, even though I didn't care all that much about it by then, because when I started walking to get my books and purse off the table everything looked blurry. My legs got shaky and I sat back down. Linda just kept hanging around looking sorry for me. "It's no big deal," I told her. "What does this school know?"

"That's right," she said, "it's only a popularity contest." What made it so cruel is that it just popped out, so I knew it was what she really thought. She didn't mean to rub it in that I wasn't popular enough to win, but that's what she did, and it made me feel completely alone.

This Narrative B does just what it's supposed to do. First of all, and most important, for six paragraphs the writer takes on a personality not her own, seeing and telling about an experience vividly and coherently enough to make it seem real. The thoughts and feelings aren't actually Kim's, of course. Kim would have her own version of the incident to tell. But what counts is that they are not Linda's. Linda, the actual author, has been demoted to supporting actor status. As Kim, she looks at this "Linda" entirely from the outside. The proof that she's really into the part comes when she shows she can view Linda with indifference, even scorn. It's a most promising sign in beginning fiction writers if they can see how their well-meant words or acts could be considered mean or ugly by others.

But although we get Kim's very different view of things in this version, it's clear that her account is based on the same set of data that Linda presented in Narrative A. The vitality of Kim's narrative springs in large part from the energy of those painful actual events she shared with Linda. Most of what Kim recalls can be confirmed by Linda's account. Even when it can't be, we still feel that Kim's version is based in the same data as Linda's. So when Linda *as* Linda wrote Narrative A, to have mentioned her own red sun dress would have seemed both vain and petty. But it feels right for Kim to remember Linda as an unwelcome flash of red, annoyingly hot. Their being each other's campaign managers is also an intriguing addition in Kim's version of the incident, and again not a surprising omission from Linda's. Linda wouldn't want to remember she'd managed Kim's losing bid, whereas Kim would be just as sure not to forget she'd managed Linda's win.

Kim's narrative depicts a character that agrees with the personality profile made up from the checklist. Kim is clearly aggressive, individualistic, insecure, sharp-witted, and suspicious. It's not hard to imagine her being impulsive and willful as well. The writer has done an excellent job of finding (or possibly even inventing) details that reveal the qualities she picked to focus on. She has made a set of abstract characteristics show themselves in specific actions. So the essential outline of a fictional character or "persona" has been staked out. What remains is to fill it in, give it color.

Finally, Kim's Narrative B seems even more tense and agitated than did Linda's Narrative A, more "unstable" and in need of resolution. Movement away from this crisis point seems absolutely necessary, even if the direction of the movement isn't fully clear. The action seems to push us forward toward future consequences, to some point where Kim's frustration will surface in some interesting conclusion which our author can describe for us.

• four •

TRANSPOSITION

WHAT DO YOU MEAN, TRANSPOSITION?

Writing Narrative B freed you from the confines of your own personal experience. You stepped out of your familiar identity and into someone else's. That step took you from the world of autobiography into the world of story. The difference between writing about your actual self and writing about an invented self is the difference between confession and fiction. It is the essential act of *distancing*, which draws a line between the straight diarist on the one hand and the conscious artist on the other. Everything you write on the "artist" side of the line will be fiction.

You could continue composing in your present masquerade costume, pretending to be "B." You might well end up with a short story. But to make your success much more certain, you're going to do another distancing act. Technically it's called switching the point of view. Mechanically it means changing all the first-person pronouns to third-person, so that every *I* becomes *he* or *she*, every *me* becomes *him* or *her*, every *we* becomes *they*, etc. It *transposes* the whole angle of presentation.

But before you start altering your own copy, go back to chapter 3 and read the sample Narrative B there. Then immediately read the following transposed version (Narrative B2), to feel how much difference a few pronoun changes can make in a narration's effect.

Sample Narrative B2

Somewhere between "a hill blossoms in green and gold" and "there are dreams" Mr. Smith's harsh tones crackling over the intercom stopped the girls chorus' feeble attempt at "Somewhere My Love." Kim had been waiting for this moment for months, ever since Linda and she had decided they'd get themselves elected to student council. Linda was Kim's campaign manager, and Kim was Linda's. So they were each working as hard as they could to get them both in.

There it was, Linda's name! She'd made it—all right! Now all Kim had to do was wait for her own name. Mr. Smith was bound to say Kim. He'd never cared for her, she knew, but he didn't pick student council winners. He might not like her style, but the junior class knew her, knew she was the right one for this job.

But then why wasn't her name called? Was Mr. Smith really taking it out on her for wearing noisy shoes from Hong Kong that clattered in the halls? Who was it that counted the ballots—Mrs. O'Connell? She'd be glad to cheat her if she got the chance. All this stir about her, what was going on? Congratulations, Julie! Way to go, Linda! What about Kim? But nobody even remembered Kim was in the running. All she could think was, "I can't believe it."

Then she felt a hand on her shoulder and saw Linda out of the corner of her eye. Who was she to come and console her? Kim wanted to scream at her, "You don't know what it is to lose, in your silly red sun dress. Everybody thinks you're just terrific, because you're just *like* everybody. Oh, get away, I don't need your gloating sympathy!"

Kim could tell she'd started crying, even though she didn't care all that much about it by then, because when she started walking to get her books and purse off the table everything looked blurry. Her legs got shaky and she sat back down. Linda just kept hanging around looking sorry for her. "It's no big deal," Kim told her. "What does this school know?"

"That's right," Linda said, "it's only a popularity contest." What made it seem so cruel to Kim was that it just popped out, so she knew it was what Linda really thought. She didn't mean to rub it in that Kim wasn't popular enough to win, but that's what she did, and it made Kim feel completely alone.

Except for the pronoun substitutions and a few minor rewordings to make the sense of something clear, Narrative B2 is identical to Narrative B. But these small changes in wording make a big change in the way readers "hear" the account. In Narrative B somebody named Kim told her own version of an experience with all the vigor of direct recall and the conviction of life relived. In Narrative B2 an anonymous third-person narrator is in charge, making a cooler, more objective presentation that puts space between us and the action.

We know that Kim in Narrative B isn't real the same way Narrative A's Linda is, yet they both seem to address us "live," face to face, unhampered by any transmitting apparatus. In B2, information comes by way of a fleshless, faceless voiceover from off stage that controls the pitch and tone of the action, regulates the whole mood of the show. This mysterious narrator is in fact you, "the author." With a few flourishes of the pen you've done a bloodless coup, seized absolute power of life and death over every citizen in your storyland.

It may leave you feeling a little like the candidate who, when elected, asked his staff, "What now?" Considering all the advantages of first-person narration that you've just given up, mightn't it be wiser to hand the job right back to B? Who's in a better position to tell B's story, after all, than B? What's wrong with telling a story in first person? Aren't some of the world's best stories in first person?

Yes, they are, and nothing's wrong with using first person—it just requires more skill than you probably have yet. This question of "point of view" is a large and fairly complicated one. But it has to be asked, *and answered*, because it's important for you to know why your story will be told in third person rather than first.

WORKING IN A STRAITJACKET

First of all, you can't really get rid of your responsibilities as author of your story. Using a fictitious character like B to tell it might seem to free you from having to take charge. Just let B do the talking. You can hide behind B and avoid committing yourself. But ask yourself: when the ventriloquist's dummy talks, who doesn't know where the voice comes from? Characters are an author's dummies. If he doesn't work them, they don't work. He may choose to let them speak for themselves or to pass along what they say in summary or paraphrase. Regardless, he is accountable for every syllable his characters utter. So telling a story in first person doesn't *gain* a writer freedom, it loses him freedom by forcing him to speak constantly in a single character's voice, that of his "persona," his talking dummy.

Since a first-person account is bound by its narrator's scope, grasp, and range of expression, the meaning of such an account will depend on what its narrator sees, understands, and relates. Of course, just as a skillful ventriloquist voices personal opinions through his dummy, a skillful author makes a first-person narrator speak for him. But he must take care not to let his dummy/narrator talk in a way his audience/readers will find "out of character." If the dummy mouths words that clearly don't belong to him, it's like seeing the ventriloquist's lips move.

Unlike the ordinary puppet master who sits and chats with a dummy on his knee, the writer of a first-person narrative can't afford to appear "on stage" at all. If he does, the whole effect of letting the persona/character tell the story is spoiled. Everything must appear to come from the narrator. If the narrator can't seem to manage the story on his own, an author is going to feel tempted to rush to his aid with a few well-chosen words of clarification or insight. But a first-person narrator's freedom of expression is sacred. He must be allowed to muddle through on his own, with only such prompting as his author can provide from off-stage.

Another complication in using first-person narrators is that they know the end of the story before they even start telling it. Say a narrator begins: "I walked up the path and knocked on the door. A woman opened it and asked what I wanted." Because the account is presented in past tense ("walked," "knocked," "opened," etc.) we know at once that all its action has already occurred and the narrator is simply telling us how he remembers it happening. This "foreknowledge" a first-person narrator has can make his author's life miserable.

Imagine such a persona telling a murder mystery. What's going to be the very first thing he wants to shout? Right: "The butler did it!" Muzzling a fractious dummy without seeming to interfere with his freedom of expression has been known to defeat the patience and skill of many a practiced writer. One way of gagging a narrator is to impose present tense on him. If he has to say, "I walk up the path and knock on the door. A woman opens it and asks me what I want," he no longer enjoys the wisdom of hindsight and has to wait with the rest of us to see what happens next. But this is a drastic solution that usually makes more problems than it solves. First-person point of view is so "hot" and bright all by itself that the extra hype of present tense is enough to send most stories into stylistic overload.

First-person narrators also have a hard time reporting themselves and their behavior fairly. If not abnormally self-critical, they will tend to see themselves as acting always with the best of motives. If not abnormally conceited, they'll play down their own heroics. If not downright vain, they'll never call themselves "handsome" or "glamorous." First-person narrators can't even comment on their own thoughts without sounding self-important. The difference in effect between "I said earnestly" and "he said earnestly" is slight, but crucial. "I said" is *subjective*, "he said" is *objective*. Consider the implications: *objective* equals credible and accurate; *subjective* equals dubious and unreliable. Since part of a fiction writer's job is to create a believable illusion of reality, first-person narration is actually written "against the grain," whereas third-person narration goes with the grain. Given all the potential pitfalls, it's no wonder that successful self-characterizations are so rare.

Of course great stories have been written in first person. Great artists have always responded to great challenges. In *The Sound and the Fury*, Faulkner proved it was possible for an idiot—with a lot of help from his author friend—to tell a complex story. If the puppet-narrator Benjy didn't have a ventriloquist as skillful as Faulkner working him, he wouldn't get very far. Benjy's monolog is in fact an exceptional tour de force of storytelling craft that simply proves the rule: the narrower your narrator's field of vision, the more peculiar and/or distorted his perspective, the harder will be the author's job of getting the story out. Faulkner deliberately chose to handicap himself, knowing he would have to use all his technical skill to make up for Benjy's shortcomings as a narrator. Experienced writers can risk technical hazards knowing they have the ability to cope. Beginners should be wary of such experimentation until they have learned the basics of fictional technique.

A COMPROMISE SOLUTION TO THE POINT-OF-VIEW PROBLEM

If first-person narration can feel like a straitjacket, why not reject all restrictions on what you can see and report? Isn't it a mistake to give up omniscience if you don't have to? Unhappily you do have to. You may declare you're going to know everything that's going on everywhere in your story's world, including what is happening in every character's mind, but you can't possibly report everything your all-seeing eyes see. It'd be like counting, one by one, the grains of sand on a beach—you'd never be done. You'll have to sacrifice some of your omniscience and be selective about the details you include, if you want to write a "short" story. And since you must retreat, might as well make it an orderly retreat to a strategically sound position—the single perspective of one central character. This will shrink that vast ocean of data down to swimming pool size and make for a focused presentation that will feel personalized, like actual life experience.

But, you object, doesn't this put me right back in that straitjacket I just got out of? Granted, it does restrict your view of things to what a solitary pair of eyes sees and an individual mind thinks, but by staying in the third-person narrative mode you avoid the worst of the first-person confines. For one, third-person narration rids you of the recollection trap. Readers will let you as author take liberties they won't allow you as ventriloquist. If a first-person dummy knows the butler did it, being only a dummy he's going to want to blab. But if a third-person author-narrator knows it, readers not only allow him to keep the secret but expect him to do so, for the good of the story, until solution time in the final chapter. This freedom to keep the cat in the bag, to choose when and how to let it out, comes in very handy whether yours is a mystery story or not.

By not having to speak the story in your main character's own voice, you can also slip in much about that character that he or she would find it awkward to say. First-person narrators can't tell us straight out what they look like, so they're always meeting themselves in mirrors, train windows, reflecting pools, and trying to note down, as unselfconsciously as possible, what they see there. In third-person mode you can report such information as "straight white teeth" or "long blond hair" without sounding pompous. Even more importantly, you can record long conversations without making readers wonder about your incredible memory.

From your neutral position between character and reader, you can give the reader a fairer picture of the character than he could himself. This appearance of objectivity and the feeling of reliability that it produces are the greatest assets of third-person coverage. By being able to use reader trust to help you along instead of having to wonder how to compensate for reader skepticism about an unreliable first-person narrator's version of things, you can pay more heed to getting the substance of your story right and worry less about the technical side of sending a clear message.

Because readers trust you, you can sneak in all sorts of manipulative nudges. Of course you're bound not to misrepresent your point-of-view character's actual attitude. If you start slanting your presentation so conspicuously that readers feel you aren't being fair to your character's motives and beliefs, you lose your authorial immunity and become a sort of unreliable first-person narrator yourself. But within these limits, you can get away with lots of "subliminal" suggestion.

One of Hemingway's best-known stories, "A Clean, Well-Lighted Place," shows how an author can use his "objective" third-person status to stack the deck in favor of the thesis he's urging. Hemingway wants us to respect the old cafe waiter's fear that life may, after all, have no meaning. His strategy is to play strongly and tellingly on our emotions. First he describes a pathetic, deaf old man drinking brandy to while away the late-night hours. The old waiter is concerned about the old man's welfare, but the young one is indifferent, even hostile to him. He tells the old man he should have killed himself and deliberately overpours his brandy so it slops down the stem of the glass. He even tells the old waiter, "An old man is a nasty thing." But far and away the most emphatic signal from the author comes when the young waiter tells the old man he must leave:

> "Finished," he said, speaking with that omission of syntax stupid people employ when talking to drunken people or foreigners. "No more to-night. Close now."

Hemingway is instructing us to dislike this young man. By contrast the old waiter is shown to be gentle and compassionate:

> "I am of those who like to stay late at the cafe. . . . With all those who do not want to go to bed. With all those who need a light for the night . . . Each night I am reluctant to close up because there may be someone who needs the cafe."

No doubt about who deserves our trust, whose creed Hemingway is asking us to accept as honorable. Unless we choose to reject our author's guidance, there's only one allowable interpretation of the story. Hemingway says, as Tennyson had before him, that "there lives more faith in honest doubt, /Believe me, than in half the creeds." When we have time to reflect on this message, we may decide we don't accept it. But while we're in the grip of the story, Hemingway coaxes both our reason and our feelings into going along, at least temporarily, with his moral code.

On balance, then, this compromise point of view—"limited" or "restricted" third-person—provides the best balance of flexibility and control for beginning writers, which is why you'll be using it for your first story. But don't get the idea it's like having training wheels on your bicycle. Many of the most delicate and sophisticated stories ever written are in the "limited third" mode. Because of its overall serviceability, it remains the point of view most commonly used by serious fiction writers.

As you practice using it yourself, you'll begin to get a feel for the author's dual linkup—on one hand with the story, on the other with the reader. Despite all the experiments in story-writing technique over the years, the basic stance of the story writer stays the same: with a wonderful magic lantern, the author screens a series of pictures for us so fascinating our attention is caught and held spellbound. While we sit there, helplessly agape, the author runs his commentary over our unsuspecting ears, relentlessly guiding our reactions to what we see, helping us to understand its proper meaning. This method of reader management, which must date back to some stone-age cave gathering, lets the teller dramatize a story and interpret it all at once. For writer and reader alike it's the most nearly fail-safe narrative scheme available.

• five •

MAGNIFICATION

THE NEXT TRANSFORMATION

Four chapters done, and your project doesn't much resemble a finished story. Just one page, and you may not care much for the looks of that page as the basis for your story. It may be hard for you to believe, but you're making progress at just the rate you should. With this chapter you're actually halfway there. A story normally grows like a child in the womb, slowly at first as its unique features start to differentiate, then at a steadily quickening rate during the latter half of the gestation period.

In fact this lesson alone will actually triple the bulk of your embryo story. But even though your one page will become three, your story won't end up a single minute longer. You are going to *expand* your summary into a scene, but not *extend* the time period it spans. Put another way, you will take three times the space to cover the same events already narrated in B2. Beginning writers anxious to get on with the further adventures of their character sometimes ask at this point, Haven't we stayed with this one piece of action long enough for now? Why not leave B2 alone a while and turn our attention elsewhere?

The answer is that B2 isn't in a fit state to be left alone yet. If you've done your work well, it's probably a very good summary, but it still doesn't have the look and feel of a short story, or even a short story segment. As is, it makes a coherent presentation that any reader should be able to follow. But it's unlikely to raise anyone's blood pressure. It doesn't take us into its world and make us experience its events.

The reason is easy to see—it lacks the density, the solidity of real life. It is *told* rather than *shown*, summarized rather than dramatized, so that it feels second-hand rather than first-hand, and lacks the vividness and vigor necessary to hold readers in the spell of its "reality." It doesn't matter that your readers know your fiction is invented. They can't suspend their disbelief (see the discussion of this in chapter 3, "What the Reader Expects"), however willing they may be, unless you give them a convincing alternative world to visit.

WHAT THE MAGNIFYING GLASS REVEALS: DETAILS

One big reason your Narrative B2 seems pale and vague compared with the red-blooded meat of raw reality is that it lacks body. The way you remedy this is by putting flesh on the skeleton, filling in the empty spaces between the bones with details. A newspaper photo or television picture is really nothing more than a mass of dots. The more dots per square inch, the sharper the image. What you are about to do is put in enough dots to make a quality picture.

The principle is elementary. If you are told you are in a room, you could be millions of different places. But if you are told as well that it's a *living* room, more than 90% of possible rooms are eliminated at one stroke. If the living room also contains a blue sofa, over 90% of possible living rooms would be disqualified. If that blue sofa has a teakwood coffee table in front of it, surely at least 99% of living rooms with blue sofas would fail to fit the description. With enough detail, you can narrow anything down to the point of uniqueness. Being specific means that you notice the singular particulars of things rather than their general qualities. Since life happens uniquely and individually to each of us, the closer a story comes to happening that same way the more "real" it seems, the more "lifelike."

The illusion of reality that occurs when sensory data bombard a reader's senses (sight, hearing, smell, taste, and touch) is often said to be an *absolute* virtue of fiction writing, something always to strive for, regardless of other considerations. To say *always* is risky. Exceptions always seem to pop up. But it's almost surely fair to claim that most failed fiction—in fact most bad writing generally—fails in power and point because it lacks the grit and heft of "documentary evidence" to give it substance.

But just as you were selective in choosing that bit of your life for Narrative A, so you must be selective in the details you now choose to flesh out B2. Piling up data at random won't serve your purpose. A trash heap is still a trash heap, regardless of size. From the countless details that actually make up the events of B2 you must pick out the few that will best show readers what it was like—or more precisely, what you want them to feel it was like. You remember the Fiction Contract: Everything in a story happens according to its author's purpose. That means literally *everything*. All your story's evidence, however objectively presented, should help you make your story's case.

So you must be mercilessly practical in choosing your details. It's not enough for them to be quaint or pleasant or inoffensive. They must be *useful*. Anything less is deadwood, and deadwood will only puzzle the reader's understanding with its irrelevancy. Since all irrelevancy, however charming, must be excluded from the final version of your story, the wisest policy is not to let it in to begin with. If you let your fancy roam free, it may well come up with all sorts of delightful decorations that have nothing whatever to do with your story's purpose. Parting with such baubles can be painful after they have worked their way into your heart.

Very rarely a roving imagination may catch onto some bit of fluff that has a relevance invisible to logic, but your story will suffer more than it will benefit from a reliance on such "inspiration." Tell yourself firmly that a random detail is a fictional weed, that a rose in the cabbage patch is a weed just as surely as a dandelion is, and that you'll keep your cabbage patch free from both roses and dandelions. But even such rejected data can be useful to you. What doesn't belong is often a good clue to what does. So think carefully about any weeds you discard. What is it that makes them weedy? If they're weeds, what are cabbages? What is my patch all about? What's my "case"?

You may feel you have to admit that you don't yet really know what your story's case is. Don't spend time just now fretting about the specifics of your story's theme and thesis. At this stage let your case be simply to sketch a convincing portrait of your main character as an "actual" person living in a "real" world, dealing with a significant crisis in an understandable way. Your coverage should serve to reveal this character's view of B2's events in particular and life in general. In the process, of course, you will also define your own attitude toward the character's views.

THE PROTOCOL OF FICTION

Your own attitude? Exactly. What you want your story to *say*. As explained back in chapter 3, fiction is a form of *persuasive* writing. Readers expect you to know this and to live up to your half of the Fiction Contract. But they also expect you to understand its primary proviso, the article of Fictional Protocol:

> No matter how determined an author may be to sell his ideas, he *never sells direct.*

This protocol is so well established that today's readers need no one to tell them "the moral of the story" is never spelled out in so many words. A story is a story, a sermon something else—two different forms of discourse, each with its own guidelines. Readers won't be preached at in a story. Not that they're irreligious or unwilling to learn. They may accept straight moral advice from the likes of Ann Landers or Billy Graham. And they don't object to moral lessons in their stories either. In fact readers expect most fiction to carry some sort of message. But it must be left to them to find or feel or figure, not be crammed down their throats. The moral for writers is clear: If you want readers to get your point, neither you nor anyone in your story can speak it, *or even think it*, in so many words.

This protocol will help you choose the most useful details for encouraging readers to see the picture as you want them to. It's a constant reminder of the need for subtlety, grace, and tact. And those aren't just polite words for fraud and deception, either. Writers must play totally fair with their readers. A good guide never misleads faithful followers. Each step along the path holds clues to your story's final point, and it is your job delicately to bring their significance home.

As an example of how much an author can and cannot get by with in the way of telling the reader what to think, let's say you want to suggest that the Establishment often manipulates the will of the individual. You picture your "individual" waiting in the coldly impersonal reception room of a bureaucratic office. He notices a spider's web on the legs of the metal chair opposite him, sees a fly struggling helplessly in it. He may even feel sorry for the fly's predicament. But if the author goes beyond that to actually comment on how the fly's situation mirrors the character's, the author is "selling direct" and has gone too far.

STRIKING THE RIGHT BALANCE

Our fly in the spider web is a physical detail that, when seen by the character in the waiting room, prompts a thought in his mind. This thought is a conceptual detail with no sensory reality—it can't be seen, heard, smelled, tasted, or touched. But such insubstantial data are just as consequential as the more material ones. Sensory evidence is of course essential. Readers can't enter a world that has no air to breathe or ground to walk on. The hard, physical existence of rooms and furniture must be established. But you must never forget that a main concern of your story must be to follow the progress of your main character's changing attitude. Meaning that much of it will take place inside your character's head, where no sensory data are available. If a character sees a fly caught in a web, readers want to know how that registers in his mind, where the most vital business of the story is happening.

This alternation between inner and outer events is one of the unique qualities, and strengths, of fiction. Drama is pure showing without telling—thoughts are revealed only when spoken. Essays, except for rare bits of embedded anecdote or parable, are telling without showing. Only fiction has the flexibility to move easily back and forth between showing and telling, scene and summary. As a fiction writer you have a responsibility to make the most of your genre's special capability. This means keeping your coverage balanced, never losing sight of either the external environment—the physical world actions occur in—or the internal thread of your central character's thought processes.

CHOOSING AND MANAGING INTERIOR DATA

What internal evidence deserves to be included? The short answer to that is of course the *relevant* evidence. But that's really just another question—what's relevant? And you're not yet in a position to answer that question fully. Later, when you've come to a better understanding of what your story is all about, you'll most likely need to return to this segment and fill in some of the blank spaces in your character's inner life. But for now you should go back to that personality profile you did for B in chapter 3 and check it against your Narrative B2 to see how well B2 does at revealing the bundle of characteristics you picked out to emphasize. Note down any discrepancies between the way B behaves there and the way he should behave based on the personality profile you did. You should be able to explain all such discrepancies, so that your readers won't feel that B's conduct is either inconsistent or unconvincing.

Where to hunt for interior data to expand B2? First of all, go back and walk yourself through the actual experience once more, as B, but also as the holder of that checklist of personal characteristics/personality profile on B which should help you turn up some possibilities for added coverage. It may even stir your memories of the incident enough to bring up fresh, relevant information. But however good your memory, your imagination is going to have to be better. From this point on, your case will be built mainly from "facts" you fabricate in your own idea factory.

What you're working toward is "character independence," the capacity of a fictional person to run on his own. Once you've fed enough data bits into a character, he quits being a concept and becomes a "live" entity, one who seems able to walk, talk, and think for himself, who doesn't need you to make him go, put words in his mouth, notions in his head. You may have to start setting limits to what he can get by with (even so, he's likely to break your rules), but your main job comes down to standing by ready to jot down whatever he says or does.

The mechanics of jotting down interior data can be cumbersome. As with any skill, you'll need lots of practice before you can make interior drama flow smoothly. But here are a few guidelines:

1. Report most of what happens "inside" indirectly. That is, instead of quoting thoughts word for word, paraphrase them.

    So: Kim could tell she'd started crying . . .
    Not: Kim thought, "I've started crying . . ."
    Or: What made it seem so cruel to Kim was that it just popped out, so she knew it was what Linda really thought,
    Not: Kim felt, "What makes it so cruel is that it just popped out, so I know it's what she really thinks."

2. Even when citing thoughts directly, it's usually best not to put them in quotes. Quotation marks give words an oral quality that has to be explained if the words aren't actually voiced. All such nonvocal speeches have to be tagged "he thought" or "she wondered" in order not to confuse the reader.

    So: Who was it that counted the ballots—Mrs. O'Connell?
    Not: "Who was it that counted the ballots—Mrs. O'Connell?"

    And a simple *She couldn't believe it* would probably serve our sample story better than that complicated *All she could think was, "I can't believe it."*

3. Underscoring words in manuscript means italicizing them in print. Either underlining or italics gives words an extra intensity that may be too strong for most thoughts. Of course

sometimes italics can be very helpful to a writer trying to do a tricky job of sorting out different kinds of interior data for the reader. Italics can also be used to distinguish interior from exterior data in a passage that alternates rapidly between the two. The effect is something like a voice-over:

> The noise of the machinery came at her from all sides. *I can't think.* The deep roar of huge engines, the clatter of drive chains, the harsh grinding of metallic plates and arms . . . *I've got to get out of here.* She tried to retrace her steps, but found she was lost in the maze of turnings. She began to run. *If I don't escape soon . . .* Plunging headlong toward the center of the noise, louder, louder . . . *I can't take it.*

The main point to remember in presenting interior data is that it is the least "natural" form of reporting in fiction. You have to use your special author's probe to get at this inside information, so you'll need to take extra care to keep that operation from getting in the way of the reader's view of the picture you are painting. Of course the reader wants to trust you and believe in your fictional world. What you have to do is not to forfeit that trust. The guidelines given above for reporting interior data are all intended to help give your coverage a straightforward and accurate look. If you can tell your readers what your main character is thinking without calling attention to yourself you can consider your handling of interior data successful.

CHOOSING AND MANAGING EXTERIOR DATA

Exterior data are chosen on the same principle as interior data. To deserve inclusion a detail must be useful in some way to the story at large. All weeds must go. Everything that stays has to contribute. Put another way, your story is a team effort and the details are your team. Like so many ants or bees, they must all work for the good of the common project. Any detail that either stands idle or draws attention to itself rather than the story as a whole just doesn't belong. Which is why there are no red herrings in a well-crafted fiction. Each sentence moves the story forward by providing some new development in the progress of its argument toward a conclusion. Not that every sentence has to contain some fresh twist in the plot. Sometimes a story's progress is better served by a quiet description than by a feverish rush of activity. But the basic principle remains: everything has to mean something, count for something.

This may seem to impose severe restrictions on your creative "freedom of choice." Granted, it clips your wings a bit, but only a bit. Regard it as another voluntary reduction in your authorial power and responsibility. By giving up the right to include just anything life happens to throw your way, you earn the chance to take the shaping of life's materials into your own hands. Rather than making do with the rough, raw, and random stuff of real life, you get to improve it up to the level of art. This practice of improving on life gave fiction writers a bad name in bygone days, when puritanical types thought any kind of playing with truth was sinful. Luckily for both storyteller and general public, it's now generally conceded that the act of writing fiction isn't in itself either moral or immoral. Stories are well- or ill-crafted, serve good or bad goals, depending on the skill and virtue of authors. But the storyteller's right to enhance the facts of experience is no longer disputed.

When you start casting about for exterior data to fill out the skeleton framework you set down in B2, how are you going to know the relevant from the irrelevant? Part of the job of exterior data is to build the visible world in which the action of your story takes place. So it might be argued that whatever makes that world seem real is relevant. The problem is, relevance itself is relative. Of all possible useful data some are more useful than others. In a short story there's only room for the most useful.

The most useful exterior data are those that help clarify your main character's mental attitude and the change in it which your story records. This is why a writer might choose to pay attention to a spider web on a chair's legs rather than spending time on a description of the chair itself. The chair is there, along with hundreds of other objects, ready to be described as part of the waiting room. All are therefore in their way "relevant." But the web gets chosen because it helps in more than one way. It implies the room's untidy and run-down look. But it also suggests the main character's mood of hopeless desperation.

A rule of thumb, then, for picking exterior data: look for what will engage your reader's senses in the action and at the same time reflect the status of your main character's feelings. The sample Narrative B2 already contains several such details: Mr. Smith's voice is "harsh" and "crackling" over the intercom. He dislikes Kim's "noisy shoes from Hong Kong." Linda's red sun dress is "silly." Naturally this summarized scene's physical environment still feels pretty sketchy, but at least the data given are well charged with the central character's outlook.

The point to keep in mind at all times is that everything you report is slanted by the viewpoint of your character, the author of Narrative B. Even though you've taken over the job of official narrator by transposing from first-person to third, you're still bound by the eyes and ears, as well as the heart and mind of B. B's personal bias functions as a kind of filter over your recording camera lens. The objective evidence must be put through the subjective filter of B's perspective. The story sees both what and how B sees.

Of course most of the time B's slant won't skew reality all that much. B needs to have a well-enough balanced view of the world that readers can regard B's perception and account of things as generally reliable. No Poe lunatic or Faulkner idiot should twist the heart of your first story. But like any other "normal" person, B does have defects of vision and judgment, and these should be employed to your advantage. While his overall reliability will help establish how things really are, you must use his subjective fallibility to flag the nature and extent of the psychological hazards he faces. This variable subjectivity factor is another of fiction's most useful resources, one you must be prepared to exercise to the full.

THE MOST IMPORTANT KIND OF EXTERIOR DATA

Of all the bits of evidence you amass in building your story's case, none is more vital than dialog—the quoted speeches your characters make. So why do beginning writers seem to shy away from reporting conversation? The commonest reason given is simply not knowing quite how to punctuate it. But that problem is so easily solved by taking a look at how dialog is punctuated in published stories, it seems learners are really looking for an excuse to avoid writing dialog. When pressed, most learner fiction writers insist that there's just something about dialog that makes them uncomfortable and causes them to handle it awkwardly.

But why? The average person spends far more time listening to other people talk than watching sunsets, so why should beginning writers feel more comfortable painting a scene than recording a conversation? For one thing, years of English classes taught us all to use grammatically correct prose, and spoken language doesn't play by the same rules so it's hard to capture. Then, too, good fictional dialog isn't just a matter of making believable transcriptions of human speech. But whatever the reason for the problem, and no matter how much you may want to avoid dealing with it, you may as well make up your mind to start tackling it right now. There's no getting 'round the need for dialog in fiction. It's simply one of the skills you need to acquire, and like any other acquired skill, once you have it you'll enjoy using it.

As for overcoming the weight of ground-in grammar and "proper" usage, the first key to freedom is realizing that your cell is unlocked. When you put quotation marks around a sentence you are saying that sentence is to be read as spoken. And spoken not by you, the author, but by someone else whose words you have a duty to report as uttered, not to correct. So even if you feel that you personally ought to stick to the rules you learned in school, you can't afford to make your characters talk the way you write. With dialog, hearing is believing. If readers can't hear your people talk, they can't believe anything else about them either. A character who doesn't talk human simply isn't human.

Knowing that all quoted material has to sound like speech, you can probably predict the next step: speak it. Yes, out loud. Too embarrassing, talking to yourself? Sorry, but if you're going to write fiction, you'll need to get over that inhibition. Of course you can probably get others to help you out by listening to you read finished speeches. Maybe they'll even read your dialog back to you. Hearing someone else recite your dialog often uncovers flaws in it that remained hidden from your ears when you spoke it yourself. But however much help of this kind you can get, you'll still need to do a lot of talking to yourself when you are first hammering out your characters' conversations. You can't have someone standing by to read aloud every try at every speech you produce. Talk about embarrassment!

A SIMPLE EXERCISE IN DIALOG DEVELOPMENT

Typically, a patch of dialog evolves as follows: Your characters reach a point in the story where a verbal exchange is called for and you can't get by with just summarizing what they say because it's important enough to deserve word-for-word reporting. You rough out in your head what they're going to say to each other. Then you try actually sketching a few speeches on paper:

1. "What do you mean by coming in here like this?"
2. "I have come to tell you that I don't like the way we are handling the Jones contract."
3. "Why should I listen to what you think about it?"
4. "The Jones contract is important to the whole company, but my job is directly at risk."
5. "What do you feel we should be doing differently?"
6. "First, we need to centralize executive responsibility for the entire Jones operation."
7. "If you mean that you should be given total authority, you must know that no one in a corporate management structure can have that sort of power."

And so on. But we have an adequate sample for our purposes. Try talking your way through this sequence. It's supposed to sound like two people conversing. What it does sound like is bad translation or a pair of androids. Probably there are real people who actually talk that way, but it's hard to believe in them even when you see them in person. Fictional characters can't get away with being so implausible. The reader knows they're invented and so expects them to behave sensibly. When they speak, what they say should be lifelike, should have "verisimilitude." As it stands, our seven-speech conversation lacks verisimilitude. It's too neat and tidy, too grammatically complete and correct—too "good" to be true. So you knock some of the starch out:

1. "Who asked you in here?"
2. "I don't like the way we're handling the Jones contract."
3. "So you got an opinion. What else is new?"
4. "We're talking about my job."
5. "Quit belly-aching. Say what you came in to say, then get out."
6. "I think we ought to centralize executive responsibility—"
7. "Make you judge and hangman? It's a corporation, remember? Nobody gets that sort of power."

Still far from perfect, but better. What are the main differences? The most obvious one is length. "Take 1" is 100+ words, "Take 2" only 60+. Their content is roughly the same, so this is a big improvement in efficiency. "Take 2" uses contractions (like *don't, we're, it's*) to give its speeches a colloquial tone. "Take 2" also comes in short bursts that help suggest the heated atmosphere of argument. Speech 7 even cuts in on 6. Finally, as in a real conversation, the "serial logic" of the sequence feels less measured, balanced, prefab in "2" than in "1." But though we can *hear* this second conversation better than the first, we still can't *see* it. They seem to be talking in the dark. Many a modern story proves that you can have long strings of speeches without a single tag to help readers see what's happening. But unless you know you've fixed the scene firmly enough in your reader's mind to keep him in the story without reminders, it's reckless not to tag your dialog. So let's try filling in the speeches with some description.

> When Parker burst in without knocking, Moran didn't bother looking up. "Who asked you in here?"
>
> Parker's mouth opened but no sound came out. Moran looked up. Parker licked his lips and tried again. "I don't think we're handling the Jones contract right."
>
> "So you got an opinion," Moran muttered, looking down at the papers on his desk. "What else is new?"
>
> "It's my job we're talking about—"
>
> "Quit belly-aching." Moran brushed him aside with a sweeping gesture. "Say what you came in tc say, then get out."
>
> "I think," Parker began hesitantly, "we ought to centralize executive responsibility—"
>
> "—Make you judge and hangman?" Moran cut in with icy

calm. "It's a corporation, remember." He looked up, smiling. "Nobody gets that sort of power."

Back to over 100 words, but at least we now have both words and context. Probably more context than necessary, but useful for our purposes. Notice how the description is sandwiched in—before, after, and in the middle of speeches. Even more important, see how the tagwork helps pace the dialog. We can hear Parker hesitate after "I think" and Moran deliberately delay before saying "Nobody gets that sort of power." Study the technique of quotation in this passage closely. Go back to chapter 1 and look at the way Maupassant, Chekhov, and Doud handled the formatting of dialog in their stories until you begin to feel comfortable with the conventions of presenting speech in writing.

THE STUDENT SAMPLE B2 MAGNIFIED

Finally, before getting down to expanding your own B2, read the following three-page magnification of the student's B2 from chapter 4 (call it Narrative C, for Central Core). Compare C and B2 closely so as to identify the sources of C's greater density and specificity. Note that sentences from B2 have not always been kept intact. As the writer's sense of B's mind clarifies, new ways of saying things must sometimes be found. Again remember that this sample of one student's work isn't offered as a model of perfection to be copied, but as a specimen to give you some idea of how your draft might look when this phase of the process is done.

Sample Narrative C

Kim didn't know if anyone else was getting excited, but she knew she wasn't paying much attention to what they were supposed to be singing. Maybe some of the others were feeling the same way, because the chorus's rendition of "Somewhere My Love" sounded worse than lovesick that afternoon. Then just before they made it to "there are dreams," the intercom crackled and Mr. Smith's harsh voice started into its boring spiel:

"Please give me your attention, blah blah blah . . . I have an important announcement, blah blah blah . . ."

She'd told herself not to get too carried away when it finally happened, but now that the results were going to be revealed, she couldn't help tensing up. It didn't do any good telling herself to quit acting like a kid.

"I have just been handed the results of the student council election and will read the names of the elected in alphabetical order beginning with next year's seniors."

Why did he have to drag it out? Why not just admit she and Linda had made it, the way they'd planned to the last three months? Of course Mr. Smith wouldn't want to say she'd won. Never liked her style. Not dull enough to suit him. It would make winning all the sweeter.

". . . Kathy Bonner, Robert Carson, Linda . . ."

Yeah Linda! She almost shouted it out, jumping and shaking her fist in the air. Now all he had to do was say Kim, and it would all have come true. She'd managed Linda's campaign, and Linda had won. Linda had managed hers, and she'd win too. They'd both worked for each other and it was going to be a fantastic year with both of them in Council. Finally she'd get a real chance to show this school what she could do. Maybe she'd even lead a move to impeach Mr. Smith!

But now he was reading the juniors' names. All the senior class winners had been read, and he hadn't said Kim. There had to be some mistake. She and Linda were in this together. They'd asked everyone to vote for both of them. Mr. Smith might not like her wooden Hong Kong shoes that clattered in the halls when he wanted them quiet as a morgue, but he didn't pick Council winners.

It had to be Mrs. O'Connell. She probably counted the ballots, and she'd love to cheat her and give it to her pet Julie and think she was doing the school a favor.

Everyone would know if she cheated Linda, but who cared if Kim lost? No one even remembered she'd been running. Except dear Linda, of course. She'd put on a perfect sad face, like everything else she wore, and tell Kim how sorry she was for her, even though she was bubbling with joy inside because she'd won. Little Miss Favorite who never rubbed anyone the wrong way.

When Mr. Smith finished reading the list, the chorus broke up in a confusion of rushing and shouting. "Congrats, Julie!" "Way to go, Linda!" It wasn't fair, winners getting their victory and all the praise too, while losers had to eat dust and pretend not to care and join in the cheers for the winners. Kim felt the tears trying to come to her eyes and was determined she wouldn't let them out. "I can't believe it," she murmured, biting her lip. *I won't, won't cry.*

She felt a hand on her shoulder and knew it had to be Linda. The hand seemed like a lead weight pulling her down. Out of the corner of her eye she saw Linda's mask of pity and she couldn't keep the tears from coming. She wanted to scream at Linda, "Go away and leave me alone! Can't you see you're only making things worse? Don't you know you can't console me? Winners can't make losers feel good. They can only make them more miserable. It's no good pretending you care when you *can't* care. Go let the others tell you how happy they are for you and how they always knew you'd make it. Sure, you couldn't miss, in your red sun dress and sugar smile and pretty manners. Everybody's idea of perfect, because you're just *like* everybody. Go away, I don't want your gloating sympathy!"

But all she could do was cry. She wasn't going to let Linda see her tears, especially when it didn't mean all that much anyway, so she shook Linda's hand off her shoulder and walked toward the table where the books and purses were. Everything was blurred, but she didn't want to wipe her eyes. She could hear Linda behind her, and somebody shouted, "Great going, Linda!" If it wasn't for the tears, she'd turn and tell Linda where to go.

She found her purse, took out her compact and looked at herself in the mirror. No wonder they didn't vote for her if that's how she looked. She dabbed her eyes with a tissue. In the mirror Linda's dress splashed red over her shoulder. Forcing a smile, she turned around. "Congratulations, Linda. I knew you'd win."

Linda threw her arms around Kim. "Oh Kim," she moaned, "we both had to win."

So, Kim thought, I'm to blame for Linda not having a super day? Serve her right if I apologized for spoiling her fun. But Kim knew Linda didn't mean to be mean. She was too naturally sweet. So she only said, "You couldn't make them vote for me."

Linda pulled away a little, holding fast to Kim's shoulders and looking into her eyes. "Don't let it hurt you, Kim. They can't hurt you if you don't let them."

But that's just what you don't understand, Linda, it does hurt. You've never known it, never... "So who's hurting?" she said, feeling her legs go weak. She sat down, turning away. "It's no big deal.

What does this school know anyway?"

"That's right," Linda said, "it's only a popularity contest."

What made it even more cruel to Kim was that it had just popped out, so she knew it was exactly what Linda thought. Of course she hadn't meant to rub it in that Kim just wasn't well enough liked to win, but that's what she'd done, and it made Kim feel totally alone.

LONGER IS BETTER?

The time frame of this Narrative C is identical to that of the Narrative B2 it's drawn from. But it takes three times as long to tell. This means it is three times as specific, particular, and dense. It has been subjected to 3X magnification, and the result is a better picture of what really happened to Kim during those crucial few minutes. The writer has braved the hazards of dialog to give several speeches unheard in B2. But except for the added ear appeal of that dialog, not much has been added to engage a reader's senses. Most of the expansion is interior. This deficiency may not end up being a problem, especially if the rest of the story is richer in sensory data. Quite often a core episode will concentrate more on emotional values, relying on the opening scene to provide the bulk of necessary physical details.

The best of this Narrative C's invention is in the whirl of ideas its author finds in Kim's mind. The dramatic intensity of their presentation almost causes the point of view to lapse into first person. This is a real danger, not just a theoretical one. She must not lose the flexibility of third-person narration. But notice how well she succeeds in filling out her working profile of Kim. Aggressiveness shows in the shaking fist, the prospect of impeaching Mr. Smith, the loud clatter of her shoes in the quiet halls. Impulsiveness is seen in her jumping to the conclusion that Mrs. O'Connell has cheated her, her shaking Linda's hand off her shoulder, and change of heart when she suddenly turns to face Linda. Individuality is evident in most of Kim's comments, but especially strong in her scornful judgment of Linda: "Little Miss Favorite who never rubs anyone the wrong way." Insecurity reveals itself in her suspicion of Mr. Smith and Mrs. O'Connell.

Sharp-wittedness is apparent throughout—when she calls the chorus's singing worse than lovesick, gives Mr. Smith's words as blah blah blah and claims he wants the high school to be a morgue, says Linda is naturally sweet, and even when she sees herself in her mirror and tells herself it's no wonder they didn't vote for her if that's what she looked like. Willfulness in this scene comes mainly in the form of contrariness, a stubborn reluctance to behave predictably.

All told, the potential of B2 has been realized pretty fully by this enriched version of the incident. The author seems in touch with the mix of feelings and motives inside Kim and has done a competent job of conveying her status to the reader. The author's firm grip on character should provide the insight necessary to push forward to the next stage of the project.

• six •

EXTRAPOLATION

IMAGINING THE CONSEQUENCES

Before reading ahead, go back to chapter 1 and reread the section called *Where exactly is square one?* to remind yourself of the basic structure of the short story. "Readers must witness the actual turning point crisis in full." So far, so good. You have just completed a first-draft version of a full-fledged core incident. But a core is, by definition, only the heart of something. A story core is no more a story than an apple core is an apple. The whole story must show "what led up to the crisis and what happened afterward as a result. The cause and the effect. The before and the after." In terms of our line graph it means taking at least three readings—at A, at C, and at D.

You have taken your reading at "C." It is time to move on to "D" and find out what happens to your character *after* and *as a result of* the events recorded in Narrative C. This will make greater demands on your imagination than anything you have done so far, because up till now your creativity has been limited to interpreting actual experience. Of course you have had to invent—or at least guess at—the inner workings of someone else's mind. But the events of Narrative C really did happen and you really were there to see them, so that you can think back to the experience and verify the factual accuracy of Narrative C by comparing its account with the "real thing."

What you are about to do is take a leap into total fabrication. When completed, Narrative D will seem every bit as real to your reader as Narrative C does. But whereas Narrative C is a sort of rerun of a "true-life adventure," Narrative D will originate in the theater of your imagination and play for the very first time on the stage of your short story. Your task (and pleasure): inventing the future. Out of all the developments that *could* conceivably follow from the crisis of Narrative C, you will try to pick the one that, more than any other, *ought* to occur.

This means finding the continuation and conclusion that best complete and confirm the conditions set forth in the Core. But how do you know what conclusion is best? Of course you can never be positive that anything is the *absolute* best. But use the guidelines you'll be given shortly to help narrow the possibilities and apply your powers of creative speculation the way you'll be shown later in the chapter to determine the strengths of various scenarios, and you should end up with your "personal best." How near that comes to *the* best will depend on your abilities.

WHAT SHOULD HAPPEN IN A CONCLUDING INCIDENT?

First, more of a recommendation than a guideline. Narrative D is supposed to complete your weaning from the milk of real life. This means it should report events that never happened, except in your head. One way of helping to make Narrative D pure fiction is to exclude from it the character most likely to stay factual—the writer of Narrative A, yourself. You may feel that your hold on the invented reality of your story situation is totally secure, so that it's not necessary for you to take such obvious precautions. Still, the only way to prove you don't need a crutch is to throw it away. At the very least, make sure "you" are not at the center of action in the concluding episode, playing an important part in how it comes out.

In addition, the following "paired" guidelines may help you pin down the kind of development you need:

1. B's action should be consistent with what readers saw in Narrative C. Whatever B does, it should confirm the reader's understanding of B's character as shown in the Core. If it does not, the reader will reject B's behavior as implausible and refuse to accept the accuracy of your account—obviously an unacceptable loss of credibility.
2. But, at the same time, B's action must be unusual enough to be interesting, and remarkable enough to reveal some new development in B's understanding. If it isn't, the reader will start yawning and wondering why you didn't stop when you were ahead.
3. The actual change in B's outlook must be fairly slight. If it isn't, you'll probably seem to claim more than you prove—another way to forfeit reader trust. Sudden radical shifts in attitude usually result from either spiritual "revelation" or other "acts of God," or else from brain surgery, and neither of these is fiction's proper matter.
4. But the change must also seem significant in its likely consequences for B's future. It must be a "turning point" event. If it isn't, readers will feel you've given them glitter rather than real gold.

Guidelines 3 and 4 are offered to help you avoid the most dire of all reader reactions: "Oh yeah?" [#3] and "So what?" [#4].

To put this all in a sentence, B's actions following the Core Incident must stay *consistent* with his previous behavior, yet in some new way also *remarkable*, reflecting a *slight* but *significant* change in his outlook.

A LIST OF "THOU SHALT NOT"S

The above guidelines will keep you away from most plotting potholes, but there are a few specific mistakes you deserve to be warned against more explicitly:

1. Don't try disposing of B's problems by means of an accident. A story is a study of someone meeting a challenge, so that if you introduce circumstances to prevent your character from confronting his difficulties you are actually aborting the story itself. "Deus ex machina" (god-from-a-machine) solutions are

faulty not just because they are unbelievable, but because they deprive characters of their "human" right to face the consequences of their actions. Fiction isn't about good or bad luck, but the way characters respond to whatever fortune they meet.

2. Don't let B die, or even suggest he's about to die, either by his own or any other hand, or as above by accident. Unless B is almost dead when the story begins, B's death will surely be too drastic a change to satisfy guideline #3 anyway. But even if not, it's going to look like a sentimental appeal for pity or a crude attempt to shock or an easy fix for a hard problem. In any case death isn't usually much of a learning experience.
3. Don't have B wake up and find it has all been a dream. That is a cheap and lazy way to dodge responsibility for solving the story's problems. It's probably best to avoid dreams entirely. They're a very risky commodity with side effects that are hard to control. If a dream is essential to the action, be sure you aren't using it to get yourself out of a jam. Especially ugly is what can be called the Decoder Dream, which saps the life from your story by telling readers how to interpret it.
4. In fact, don't play around with your story's illusion of reality in any way. You can be tricky in future stories, after you have learned to manage normal space and time competently. For now, abide by the old so-called "unities" of Space and Time. That is, don't let B wander any great distance from the setting of Narrative C or move many hours beyond its time period. By setting such limits you establish a controlled environment for your case study. The more constant the conditions in your laboratory, the sounder your demonstration. Art is not a swindle. Illusion doesn't require deception. So keep your story straight and gimmick-free. Readers will thank you.
5. Don't introduce new issues or fresh complications into a concluding episode. If you do, you won't conclude things, you'll stir them up. You should have your hands full containing the fires of your Core incident without lighting any new ones.
6. Finally, a reminder: fiction's message is never explicit. Remember Fiction's Protocol: fiction writers never sell direct. Particularly as your story draws to a close, you may be strongly tempted to step in and help clear up any confusion. If you've followed the first guideline and made the change in B fairly subtle you may worry that it doesn't show enough for readers to pick it up. In such circumstances isn't it unnatural and unfair to have to keep this author's "vow of silence"? One of the rules of the modern short story is that nobody, neither author nor character, spells its meaning out. If you break with

the rules, you aren't playing the game. It may also help to remind yourself that readers tend to see more than you might think. Some will miss much of your meaning. All will miss some. But most are skillful, intuitive detectives capable of following a difficult trail of clues. And a few will make even more of your story than you knew was there, if you don't impose limits on their interpretive abilities.

A SAMPLE SPECULATIVE RUN-THROUGH

So much for basic do's and don't's. What if you still find yourself unable to see what happens next? How can you *make* your story's concluding episode show itself? The most reliable way of forcing fictional futures to bloom is to apply your powers of creative speculation in an adult version of that old childhood hypothesis projection game, "What if—?" From ancient cave-dwelling times to the present day, storytellers have responded to the eternal narrative question, "and then?" with this equally durable question of their own. A proper "what if?" will always answer the toughest "and then?"

Probably the finest examples of this speculative strategy at work are to be found in Henry James's notebooks and the prefaces to his collected stories, in which he offers all fiction writers, novice and journeyman alike, a series of object lessons in how to explore the potential of a story idea. His description and analysis of the origin and evolution of his own stories will always be fascinating and instructive reading for all fiction writers. The more you work at perfecting your craft, the more respectful you become of the contribution of James to the serious study of its methodology.

But let's take a sample Core of our own and try hypothesizing our way through a subsequent incident of the kind you're expected to do. Suppose B is a father who has been profiled as "ambitious," "cautious," "determined," "industrious," "self-controlled," and "stable." Suppose the Core to be a scene in which Father tells his eighteen-year-old Son that he can't use the family car because his grade report (just arrived that day) suggests he ought to spend his evenings studying rather than goofing off. Son storms out, leaving Father to wonder how he handled the situation. What next?

First of all, given his personality, what's Dad's mood likely to be, exactly? Angry, depressed, defensive, bitter? Does he feel beaten or ready to strike back? Perhaps his Boss has been critical of his work that day as well, so he's feeling more than a little sore about his own competence. And this is the time Son picks to challenge the justice of disciplinary action taken for his own good. Small wonder if Dad's mood is pretty nasty.

If his wife is handy, and less than fully supportive, he might give her a fair piece of his mind. Then, having brought her to tears without calming himself down at all, he might roar off in the car himself, pull in at a tavern, and drown himself in booze. He might even unburden himself to a fellow drinker at the bar in a soul-searching confession of his battered feelings. Plausible? It doesn't sound very cautious, stable, or self-controlled of him. But even overlooking that, it's probably not a sound continuation. Unless the scene were handled with extraordinary delicacy, Dad will turn into a whining self-made martyr who destroys the story in order to save himself. His confession would probably gut the thesis by making it too explicit and most likely lose him the reader's respect and sympathy just when he ought to be winning it. His monolog would also tend to be bombastic, sentimental, and melodramatic. On top of everything else, once he reached the tavern and started talking the scene would become physically stagnant. Measured by the four guidelines, the scene's deficiencies are very clear: Dad's whimpering confession is not *consistent* with what we know of him, the change in his manner is far from *slight*, and the display looks more like letting off steam than any *significant* lasting shift in attitude.

But that doesn't mean you've wasted your time. You're closer to finding the right continuation than you were. You know it has to be something more in line with your character's personality profile. You know that Dad should be less chatty, less self-pitying, more deserving of the reader's respect and sympathy. Just what he'll end up accomplishing is still doubtful, but your rejected scenario has helped you limit the range of possibilities. Maybe having his wife there to add to his feeling of inadequacy is loading the scene too much against him. Remove her and maybe, instead of raging out of the house, he might phone up his boss and give *him* that piece of his mind?

Such an act would prove that the argument with his son had made its mark on him. It could provide an interesting reversal of the usual "take it out on the dog" motif by sending frustration back up the line to its source instead. It might even be made to show Dad's *determination* to resist his usual *cautious* approach and to reject all petty *ambition* to assert a new *self-control*, which would cause a reader to admire his courage and self-confidence. It is at any rate a much better solution than the first one and could probably be made to work.

But it feels a bit slick, the ricochet effect too neatly ironic, like a bullet deflected back into the person who shot it. Why? Because we find it hard to believe that Dad would behave so rashly. He may be upset, but he's too steady to risk losing his job over a brief skirmish with his son. In terms of the guidelines, such behavior is neither consistent nor moderate enough to be believable. But this scenario too gives further clues to what should happen. If the quarrel with his son really is intensified by his earlier run-in with his boss, then clearly Boss has to play a part in whatever conclusion you reach. Also, by trying out the idea that Dad not leave home after the argument, you may find yourself all the more convinced that he must.

So you imagine a third continuation: After Son storms out, Dad burns inwardly and *thinks about* calling up Boss, but then thinks better of it, knowing it would be too rash. (Often the best thing to do with a near-miss scenario is to let your character consider *and then reject* it.) He drives off in the car (has he perhaps declared to Son that he needed it himself and so feels he must use it?), not knowing where he's headed, but ends up in the elite country club district outside Boss's imposing mansion. A Mercedes sits assured on the crescent driveway. Should he slash its tires? No, too extreme an act for this man. Probably not even an idea that would occur to him. But he's there. Something has to happen to make the trip necessary. Might he see, behind the curtains of a bow window, two figures gesturing violently at one another—a father and son? Again, the parallel begins to feel uncomfortable, too contrived to be plausible. It also begins to feel very much like a "fortunate" accident (#1 on the "Thou Shalt Not" List).

But why be afraid to try something exciting, even if it does seem a trifle implausible? Doesn't life get away with murder every day, and isn't fiction supposed to be lifelike? In your enthusiasm you may be forgetting that life can afford to be unconvincing. It doesn't have to prove anything, so it can be as absurd as it likes. News events often seem utterly incredible, yet we believe them. No point in not believing something that we know happened. But a fiction *is* trying to make a case, and with evidence readers know is made up. So doubts about its credibility can't be brushed off with Life's claim, "but it happened," since it didn't. Readers will be persuaded only if your evidence supports the likelihood of things happening the way you say they do. If you're still feeling reckless, best go back and read chapter 3's discussion of *Why Real Life Isn't Enough*, *What the Reader Expects*, and *The Fiction Contract*.

But if it's too coincidental for Dad to watch Boss arguing with *his* son, does that mean this whole scenario is another dead end? Not necessarily. Having Dad take off in the car and end up out front of Boss's house may feel "right" to you. If so, keep that much of it and move forward cautiously from there. What can Dad see through that window? Not much, really. Nothing dramatic. Nor peculiar. Nor wonderfully revealing. Nor can he see Boss emerge mysteriously from the house and drive off in that Mercedes, however intriguing the prospect of having Dad follow Boss's car. Anything that momentous would be such a piece of good luck that Chance would seem to smash and waste all the reserves of character analysis the story had been so carefully storing up.

So however tempting to let Dad follow Boss's Mercedes off into the night, we need something less sensational, and less of a "happy accident" to simplify Dad's problem for him. Of course, as before when an interesting continuation had to be rejected, it's possible for Dad to wish Boss would come drive off in his Mercedes. Finally, though, it must be Dad rather than Boss who does the driving off. But then why, you ask, if nothing is allowed to happen at Boss's, why bother letting him drive there at all?

The answer has to be that something does happen, something significant, but not something that comes from strange twists or surprising turns. Whatever it is must help Dad to the recognition he reaches by story's end. It mustn't be a "special event" of any sort—that is, something that seems to have waited for just the right moment, the moment Dad arrived at Boss's, to happen. No light need go on in Boss's house. But a light of some sort should dawn in Dad's head. For instance, maybe it occurs to him that he's sitting there in the dark waiting, waiting for Boss to make some move, so that he'll have something to react to.

Is that enough? Can so paltry an insight carry the burden of discovery for an entire story? The answer is, maybe. It's not enough all by itself. It will need some grace to manage the context so that the moment of discovery comes naturally and to keep Dad from making too much use of his new-found wisdom. But in principle it's a sound idea. It builds on the established foundation of plot, character, and theme, neatly (but not too neatly) knitting the two strands of Boss and Son together. It lets Dad take both responsibility and credit for tackling his problem rather than bailing him out with some artificial fix. It's about the right "size" development for the scale of the crisis, not overwhelming but not trivial either. It's consistent with his character, yet gives him a fresh insight into his life. Though slight in itself, it could be a significant discovery for him. So it satisfies the guidelines' recommendations. It involves no accidents, happy or otherwise, no death or threat of death, no dreams, no trickery, no new issues, and it offers no explicit moral. So it stays well clear of the "Thou Shalt Not" List. It just might work!

Naturally readers will want to see some results of Dad's moment of truth. What action will he take as a result of this insight? Will he apply his new understanding positively or negatively? Should such action be dramatized as part of the story's concluding scene? When should the story end, after all? Some readers are ready to quit as soon as the action stops. Others want to keep following a main character till he drops, and then attend the funeral. So you must decide for yourself just how much "follow through" is enough.

In our sample situation, some outward sign of Dad's fresh resolve should be given—perhaps no more than his turning the key in the ignition—as a way of showing, of confirming the inward change. Of course his new awareness is Dad's significant move forward. The use he makes of his awareness is frosting on your cake. Which isn't to say frosting is bad for the cake, only that you shouldn't lay it on too thick. It's important that the inner change be expressed in some sort of substantial action. That's what your resolution is all about: consequences. But if Dad decides on the spot to start living up to his responsibilities as a father by heading home for an immediate heart-to-heart talk with his son, that would be too much frosting. Remember that fiction readers actually like to help create the story's point, and that it's easier to read in what's left out than to ignore what's been put in. Better understate than overkill.

KIM'S STORY CONTINUED

Before preparing your own one-page summary of a concluding incident, read the continuation of the sample student story below. See if you can predict what's going to be said afterward about why it works.

Sample Narrative D

Kim knew it would be almost half an hour before the bus came, and she didn't want to hang around the school. She had told Linda she really couldn't take riding home with their usual gang in the car. So she started off on foot for the downtown. She could catch a public bus from there. The idea of sitting among a bunch of sweaty faceless passengers appealed to her.

The clomping of her shoes sounded louder than usual as she walked along the sidewalk at a brisk pace. When she approached the commercial part of town, the sound of her walking mixed with the street noises and the shuffle of other people's steps. She began to feel better.

A double-dip Baskin-Robbins cone pictured bigger than life against a plate glass storefront made her pause. Some chocolate mint would sure taste good. If she didn't pamper her, who would?

Two scoops please. She took tiny bites of the sweet coldness and gazed past the rainbow sherbet sign out onto the sidewalk. Handsome men in plain blue suits, motherly women in pastel dresses, high school guys in sagging Levis and smoke haloing their heads, girls in shirts with blossoms embroidered on the col-

> lars, all walking in step like an army on the move, as unhappy-looking as if they were really off to war. Wiping a trace of wetness from her cheek, she looked for a smile in the crowd. No smiles.
>
> Slowly she forced herself out of the coolness and back onto the sidewalk. It took her to the window of the Odds and Ends Shop. The poster of the flying pig was unusual. The stuffed satin heart sculptures were pretty. But the patent leather multi-color spotted belt was truly unique. It caught her eye in such an unpleasant way, and yet it caught her eye. She stepped inside the air-conditioned shop. The belt was on sale: $3.99. Of course nobody wanted to buy such a belt. She tried it on. Fit her perfectly. All its eccentricity didn't disturb her clothing. The poor belt needed her. And who could pass up such a bargain?
>
> She clattered out of the boutique holding her geometry book up against her chest so everyone could see the spectacle around her waist. A woman with mail-order features gawked at the belt with obvious disapproval, then moved along with the other desperate shoppers. Kim laughed to herself at the woman's reaction. It was exactly what she'd hoped for. Maybe she should even have "KIM" embossed on it.
>
> Waiting for the 37th Street bus, Kim leaned against a phone booth, smiling at the memory of the look of scorn on that woman's face.

Before reading on, ask yourself how effective this proposed conclusion to Kim's story seems. Does it measure up to the guidelines? Does it avoid all the "Thou Shalt Not"s?

Clearly there is no fresh crisis in this action, nothing to deflect Kim away from the direction set by the Core episode. But there is confirmation of a change, although that change is mainly a hardening of attitudes previously depicted. No matter how much Kim may insist she doesn't care what others think of her, clearly she has been hurt and is striking back at a society that doesn't appreciate her. Through her thoughts and actions, we see a stiffening of her determination to keep herself to herself and avoid depending on others for any part of her happiness. The shift in her attitude, while slight, seems likely to last.

The proposed resolution seems a fair and reasonable extension of what we witnessed in the Core. The reader isn't asked to swallow any alarming coincidences, sensational revelations, abrupt reversals, or other wild fluctuations on the reality gauge. As with the hypothetical father/son scenario discussed earlier, the conclusion confirms the Core's angle of deflection and verifies the impression given of its main character. At the same time, it offers a revealing new look at that character, allowing her to surprise us in a convincing way. As if making up for a lack of exterior data in the Core, this final scene is vivid with sensory details. In short, there seems to be a good balance of character, plot, setting, and theme, the essential elements of a successful fiction.

• seven •

DEMONSTRATION

LIKE MAGNIFICATION, ONLY DIFFERENT

You've probably already guessed your next writing assignment—to expand your one-page summary of a concluding episode into a full-fledged concluding scene of approximately three pages. In many ways it will be like the Core expansion you did back in chapter 5. You'll be filling in your sketchy account with specific details, giving its flow of events some feelable texture, enabling readers to know its external physical reality through their senses and to know the equally important inner reality of your main character's mind in their own understanding. So what you learned in chapter 5 still applies to the scene you're about to compose.

But the difference in terminology does mean a change in emphasis as well. In magnifying the Core you were concerned mainly with bringing the scene to life and making your main character's motives clear and plausible. Those remain important concerns still, and must not be neglected. But there is an additional concern to attend to. For your conclusion to succeed, it must be logically valid. It must provide a "solution" to the "problem" of the Core, and that solution must be "correct."

A short story, remember, is a piece of persuasive writing. Just as in an essay, the conclusion of a fiction must answer the questions it raises, bring its argument to a convincing close. When a geometric theorem has been properly proved, the achievement is proclaimed with the letters Q.E.D., for the Latin *Quod erat demonstrandum*, meaning "Which was to be shown." In the same way, the resolution of a good short story proves the case which the plot of the story has been steadily laying out.

Anyone who reads fiction submissions for publication will tell you that most failed stories are stories with failed endings. Painfully often, a story begins with great strength and charm, gathers force throughout its development, and seems on course for a powerful finish only to lose its momentum and direction in its closing pages, so wasting all its assembled resources. The causes of such failure are various and can be hard to pin down, but the effects are always the same: the reality of your fictional world is shattered and the validity of its thesis is nullified. If a story doesn't resolve properly, and so—in editorial jargon—doesn't "make it" or "work," no amount of noisy action or frenzied dialog can cover the flaw.

It's like working your way all through a complex math problem and coming up at last with the wrong answer. It may seem unfair for you to get no credit for all that effort. But however slight or explainable, your error isn't really defensible. As with a wrong turn into a blind alley, it can't be fudged, only fixed. Fortunately, all the planning that went into your execution of chapter 6's writing assignment should insure that your conclusion is already sound in theory. In math terms, you've got the right formula and copied the figures out correctly. What remains is to work your problem through to an accurate solution.

This means choosing details that will help clarify *relevant* qualities of the exterior environment and point up *significant* movement in your character's attitude to his/her crisis situation. As with the "magnification" of chapter 5, you will be fleshing out a summary skeleton with bits of specific data, increasing the dots per square inch on your picture. But besides *densifying*, you will also have to make sure your "proof" is fully supported. This will introduce a brand-new factor into your choice of exterior detail: symbolism. The literal level of your story—what gets presented in its actual chain of events—needs the support of a logical symbolic substructure to bind and blend its elements of plot, theme, and character into a single focused meaning. Handling symbols effectively is a challenging job, but need not be either a frightening or an overwhelming one if you understand it. Most of this chapter will be devoted to the technique of managing symbolism.

IN THE MIND'S EYE

But the need for logic affects your choice of interior data too. The all-purpose question to ask of any bit of your character's inner life before you include it is this: Will it help your readers share the feeling of change which the crisis forces on your character? In the Core incident, you used your "inside" coverage mostly to show how your character's responses to things were related to a selected set of personal characteristics. In this concluding scene (label it Narrative D for *Denouement*, meaning "unknotting"), you will need to put that same set of characteristics to the test once again, so the reader can measure the extent of change that has occurred as a result of the Core crisis.

That means you must take a fresh series of readings measuring the new status, in Narrative D, of each "index quality" your character showed in Narrative C. If your survey is both fully comprehensive and highly specific, readers will be able accurately to compare B's state of mind on the two occasions and feel that they truly do understand the nature and causes of the differences. This understanding is the source of that feeling of satisfaction all readers, from the casual to the professional, want to get from a story: the sense of having been guided through a significant chain of events in someone's life so skillfully that the experience is both lifelike in its reality and artlike in the logic of its proof and the clarity of its design.

First, then, look through your one-page summary for possible instances of "attitude recurrence"—moments when B's reactions recall earlier ones during the Core scene. Examine these parallels carefully in order to determine how much alike the attitudes are. At each parallel, ask yourself whether the change in

B's outlook, as you understand it, would tend to alter the specific reaction in question. If you feel it would not, you need to insure that the reaction is totally consistent with that in the Core, so as to emphasize that this aspect of B's character remains unchanged. But when an attitude recurrence does show a change in B's outlook you must determine the exact nature and degree of that change and devise means of revealing it *indirectly* through B's thoughts.

Let's look back briefly at our hypothetical scenario in chapter 6, the father/son confrontation. Dad is our point-of-view character, our "B." His conduct in Narrative C was supposedly drawn from six basic character traits: ambitious, cautious, determined, industrious, self-controlled, and steady. Developments in Narrative D must pick up each of these qualities and show it as either heightened or diminished or unchanged by the crisis incident. Suppose his determination and steadiness remain largely unaffected by the experience. They could be considered "control" virtues essential to his integrity as a person. They need to be shown in Narrative D, but a single instance of each should suffice to remind readers that B is basically a determined and steady person.

As for his other qualities, all might likely be affected by the experience. His ambition to join the ranks of his firm's upper management could well lose some of its luster as he learns to care more about success on the homefront. Arguing with his son could well expose weaknesses he has kept hidden for years, even from himself: his self-control may be a form of self-righteousness, his worship of hard work (industriousness) only an excuse for staying busy, his caution merely a cloak for his insecurity. Taking him to where he can actually see himself in this new light is the real business of this story, and taking readers to where they can see him make the discovery is the author's technical challenge.

What makes it a challenge is that Fictional Protocol forbids your spelling any of these developments out explicitly. The "message" of a short story must come through loud and clear, but never directly, so that ways and means must be found to *show* all these changes in B's character while never stating them outright. You probably remember that this means neither B, nor any other person in the story, can state them either, in so many words, because making characters into mouthpieces is just another try at getting 'round the prohibition against "selling direct." B will do plenty of thinking, of course, and what he thinks will help clarify the story's thesis. As long as he doesn't start telling readers what to think and so take the story's interpretation away from them, they will appreciate the guidance of his opinions.

WHO'S AFRAID OF SYMBOLISM?

Turning to exterior data brings us face to face with the subject—some might call it the specter—of symbolism. Why drag symbols in now? you may ask. We've managed to get this far without them, haven't we? Why not just go on ignoring them? Besides, isn't the use of symbolism too difficult a question to deal with in a book calling itself a "primer"? The quick answer is, we're not dragging symbols in. They have been in all along. This is the right time to discuss their use in fiction. Symbols can't be too hard for beginning writers to handle, because all story writers on every level of competence must be able to handle them.

Now, the longer answer. You don't really have any choice about whether to include symbolism in your story or not. You can either use it consciously and so calculate its effects, or you can use it unconsciously and so scatter its influence randomly. Like it or not, there are symbols in your story already, and you'll be introducing more of them with every page you write. But how can this be? How can you have been putting symbols in your story without even knowing it? That's easy. All along you've been urged to use sensory images and concrete details. Every such image or detail is also, unavoidably, a symbol.

Because a symbol is only the tangible expression of an intangible concept. We can't draw a picture of Peace, but we can draw a dove or an olive branch and say it represents peace. Sensory phenomena—like blue skies, the smell of diesel fumes, softness of baby skin, roar of heavy metal rock music—stand in for non-sensory ones—a clear conscience, industrialization, innocence, cultural alienation: that's what symbolism is. Symbols don't make things murky, they clear things up. Whenever we need to express abstract notions in a way that will communicate, we automatically resort to symbolism. Far from exotic, it's a universal practice that fiction writers share in.

To symbolize or not to symbolize—that is *not* the question. Your choice is rather between focused, useful symbols on the one hand and pointless, hence harmful ones on the other. Obviously it is better to exert some control over the effects of symbols than trust to the accidental results of symbolism running amok. The difficulty of exerting this control comes in sizing up the impact of each symbol individually and then making it fit in with the story's overall symbolic scheme. Sometimes (to make use of a little clarifying symbolism called analogy) it's like trying to harness an entire herd of horses to a single wagon. The task of coordinating them all can seem impossible. At which point you tell yourself that organization doesn't have to be complete in order to be useful, and you persevere.

SHAPING INDIVIDUAL SYMBOLS

Every part of your story's sensory world has symbolic value in the same way that water has color. What color it has depends on impurities in it and the light level and colors of its surroundings. Fictional water is more than just water. Weather in a story isn't like ordinary weather, because it happens like everything else at the bidding of the author, who makes the sun shine and the wind blow at will. A rainstorm pelts a fictional town not because atmospheric conditions happen to be right, or even because the townsfolk danced a rain dance or prayed a rain prayer or hired a rainmaker, but because rain suits the author's purposes.

There is nothing absolute about the definition of any particular symbol. The meaning of rain in a given story depends on how the author presents it. Rain has been used to symbolize fertility and vigor. It has also been used to symbolize barrenness and exhaustion. If an author makes it rain, the rain must obey the same rules other developments have to follow. That is, it must seem plausible in the circumstances and it must contribute to the whole purpose or meaning of the story. A January rainstorm in northern Minnesota is probably too unlikely an event to be fictionally useful, no matter how rich its symbolic significance might seem. In fiction, credibility simply has to come first.

A notorious breed of implausibility deserves mention in a separate paragraph. Suppose a writer says, of rain at a funeral: "Heaven wept for her." Clearly a flagrant abuse of symbolism, but what actually makes it so? Back in the last century, John Ruskin named this the "pathetic fallacy." *Pathetic* because it credits storm clouds with feeling, and *fallacy* because it falls into the logic trap known as *post hoc, ergo propter hoc*, meaning "after this, therefore because of this." You are unlikely to break the credibility rule so grossly as this, but it is a good idea to keep the dangers of "pathetic fallacy" in mind. Especially when your narrative world is supposed to seem realistic, as it is in a basic *Primer* story, you must avoid seeming to force symbolic meanings on that world. Such meanings should appear to grow naturally out of the physical environment of the story. This doesn't mean that the only good symbol is a "natural" symbol—one already present in the material before you even began thinking about symbolic meanings. But any symbol you invent and "naturalize" ought to blend in with the existing environment and seem to belong just as fully as if it had been born there.

AN ORGANIZED APPROACH TO SYMBOLMAKING

The first thing to do in building your symbolic system is to list all the bits of sensory data already written into your story. Go through the four pages of text you have composed so far and tag every use of sensory evidence. Don't bother trying to decide if the bits have symbolic potential at this point. Just note down every time one of the five senses gets called into play, regardless of its seeming significance. You will probably notice, as you do this, that you have some fairly lengthy passages totally lacking in sensory appeals. Such passages should be reviewed for possible beefing up later on. A few sensory details might reduce their abstraction level and sharpen their thematic focus as well.

In our developing student sample, the three-page Core provides very few sensory images. Several persons are mentioned, but only Kim and Linda have any physical existence. Kim wears wooden shoes and Linda a sun dress. Other "hard" data: a generic school music room containing an intercom and a table with books and purses on it. In Kim's purse, a mirror compact and a tissue. Color: only the red of Linda's dress. Sound: a brief snatch of song ("Somewhere My Love"), the crackling of the intercom, the harsh-voiced announcement, and noisy group response. Smell, Taste, Touch: none.

By contrast, the single page of conclusion already seems packed with sensory details. The clomping of Kim's shoes mingles with street noise and other people's shuffling steps. A bigger-than-life ice-cream ad on a plate glass storefront causes Kim to buy a real chocolate mint cone. The cone is sweet and cold. The ice-cream shop itself is cool. Past the sherbet sign on the sidewalk outside, Kim sees men in blue suits, women in pastel dresses, guys in Levis, smoking, and girls in shirts with embroidered collars. In the window of the Odds and Ends Shop are the flying pig poster, satin heart sculptures, and the patent-leather belt. Kim clatters out of the shop, holding her geometry book above her belt, and leans against a phone booth at the bus stop.

So much for listing it all. The next thing is to try making some sense of it by sorting it into image "families," related sets of sensory data. But related in what way? Go back to that short list of personal characteristics you drew up for B in chapter 3 and see how your imagery connects with each of the qualities you picked. You can start anywhere, but be sure to pay particular attention to recurring images. Repetition is normally an indication of significance.

In the case of Kim's story, no detail is more conspicuous than those clattery wooden shoes, which get emphasized by three separate references in the four pages. Clearly they're a mark of Kim's *individuality*, but judging from her thoughts on the way they annoy Mr. Smith with their clattering in the halls, they also show her as *aggressive* and *willful*. Is it just accidental that the shoes come from Hong Kong and the name Kim has an oriental ring? It may have been pure coincidence in real life, but in a story it serves to stress the character's exotic personality, her role as an outsider. Wearing outlandish shoes helps set colorful

Kim apart from drab Mr. Smith, the voice of conventional virtue and authority. When he announces the election results, Kim feels that her Hong Kong shoes (which make her different) have been rejected in favor of Linda's red sun dress (which makes her like everyone else). This basic opposition of wooden shoes vs. sun dress, of distinction vs. ordinariness, is the Core's main symbolic system.

In the concluding incident, Kim's shoes seem to clomp louder than usual as she walks away from school—she has to be feeling more than usually self-conscious. Nearing the downtown and mingling with other pedestrians, she feels less conspicuous. Beneath all her assertiveness, Kim is comforted by being absorbed in the crowd. Bypassing the crucial ice-cream store interval for now, we find her attention caught (in an "unpleasant" way) by the patent leather belt, which has been marked down (because, she tells herself, no one else would want it) and which of course fits her perfectly. "All its eccentricity did not disturb her clothing." It echoes and reinforces the defiant message of the Hong Kong shoes: Disapprove of me all you like, I don't want to be you! She has tried for acceptance and found she doesn't have enough of the red sun dress about her, so now she celebrates her rejection by *impulsively* buying and flaunting this "spectacle" of a belt. Note that like all good symbols, Kim's belt, shoes, and other clothing suggest meanings that agree with and support their "real-life" significance: she'll remove these pieces of her public image when she retreats to the privacy of her own bed, just as she gives up the defensiveness they represent. A story's symbolic level always affirms, never contradicts, its literal, experiential level.

What of the story's other sensory details? Do they add anything more than an enlivening tint and texture? The school intercom, a communication device, asks to be paired up with the bus-stop phone booth. The intercom brings bad news from a harsh establishment voice and draws a raucous reaction from the crowd. No sound comes from the phone booth. No one reacts to it in any way. It just stands there with Kim leaning against it, recalling with amusement the look on the face of the mail-order-featured woman. Perhaps that says something in itself—that Kim has put herself out of touch and has no interest in "communication." Unlike the shoes and belt, the intercom and phone booth form no strong link with any of Kim's short-listed personal characteristics. If the author wants readers to make much use of this potential symbol, she may need to call more attention to it.

Similarly, that table of books and purses in the Core seems to pair with the windowful of strangeness in the Odds and Ends Shop. The dull commonplace of school and all its plain futility contrast with the beautiful impossibilities of satin hearts and flying pigs. The window glass of both the ice-cream parlor and the Odds and Ends Shop lets Kim look in on wonderlands of delight, whereas the glass of her compact is a mirror that shows her herself and Linda. The geometry book, another reminder of school's tedious routine, isn't allowed to cover up her spectacular belt. But is there any significance in Kim's holding the book "against her chest"? Just a hint of insecurity?

Now as for the visit to the ice-cream parlor, it seems to trigger Kim's primary post-crisis insight. In her mood of desolation and frustration, the promise of sweetness offered by the sherbet rainbow, however artificial, calls strongly to her need for consolation and renewal. The double-dip cone, like Popeye's spinach, restores her and bolsters her confidence. It is a rationalized confidence, of course, based on a false sense of superiority to the world around her. Unlike the throng of pedestrians outside, unaware of being caught up in the tedium of life, Kim thinks she knows who she is and has the courage to be different. But maybe she's not so sure after all: is that ambiguous "trace of wetness" on her cheek telling us that she knows she too is in the march? If the wetness is really tears, Kim can't hide it from readers.

It seems that most of the sensory data in what we have so far of Kim's story does work together as a kind of symbolic network in support of a single central theme. Even the song title, "Somewhere My Love," makes its contribution to the overall effort. But the author should be aware that she sails near to the Pathetic Fallacy when she lets Mr. Smith cut off the singing just before the chorus reaches "There are dreams . . ." Mr. Smith already carries enough of a burden as "establishment tyrant" without his being asked to speak with the Voice of Doom as well. Kim must have the freedom to grapple with a human problem. If readers are made to feel that she is being persecuted by Fate and therefore fighting against impossible odds, they will have been deprived of the real drama most of them read stories for.

You may be feeling that the author of Kim's story has enjoyed exceptional good luck (just like the Linda of her story) in the way her selection of sensory detail seems to have produced exactly the sort of symbolic "message" the story needs. What the analysis of Kim's story actually reveals is that its sensory and psychological levels are in harmony. Had the two levels not supported each other, the story would have felt like a house divided against itself and could never have seemed believable. Symbols that grow organically in natural surroundings will inevitably fit in with those surroundings. The rightness of the symbolism in Kim's story isn't lucky, it's what we would expect to happen. Your four pages have grown in the same way and should contain the same sort of natural supportive symbolic material.

The most important thing to keep in mind about symbolism is that it derives straight from the known "facts" of your story situation. All the conjecture about the possible use to be made of sensory images in Kim's story did not alter the effect or meaning of what happens in it. Symbols may add weight or even depth to the thematic point a story makes, but they don't transform or contradict the message of the story's events. We don't see Kim in one way on the literal level and a different way on the symbolic level. The symbolic subtext—that unwritten message coded by your sequential series of images—doesn't make us feel that Kim's conduct is any more right or wrong than her depicted actions suggest. If we understand her more completely we may sympathize with her more fully and be more inclined to forgive her. But we don't discover suddenly, through the magic of symbolic interpretation, a solution to the riddle of her behavior. Symbolism comes as close to "selling direct" as fiction can—it's an author's way of reassuring careful readers that their understanding of a story is valid.

A SUMMARY OF PROCEDURES FOR SYMBOL SORTING:

1. Tag every sensory detail, however insignificant.
2. Separate into "family" groups of related images (like belt and

shoes, intercom and phone booth), paying special attention to *recurring* images.
3. Relate each image cluster to one or more of your main character's short list of personal qualities.
4. Assess the effects of your existing imagery so as to determine whether it provides adequate symbolic support to the "logic" of your story's argument.
5. Remedy symbolic deficiencies, building on existing images and/or discarding irrelevant ones if necessary.

KIM'S CASE CLOSED: SAMPLE DEMONSTRATION

Before reading the following expanded conclusion, go back and reread the summary in chapter 6 from which it grew. Then take careful note of the new data introduced to fill out the scene. By now you know enough about how fiction works that you can probably explain the reason for almost every addition to its mass of evidence. Which new details have been added primarily to make Kim's state of mind clearer? Which give the feeling of the action more body? Which make the logic of the argument more convincing? Which reinforce the meaning of events with a symbolic subtext?

When you have studied this sample Narrative D enough to appreciate how it becomes both more vivid and more persuasive than the summary it grew from, and can see how it accomplishes this by applying the procedures set forth in this lesson, you are ready to draft your own Narrative D.

Sample Narrative D

Kim didn't feel like standing around waiting for the school bus. Waiting was fine when you wanted to be seen, but she didn't want anybody looking at her today. So she told Linda she wouldn't be riding home with the car pool bunch. They'd be so sympathetic it would make her barf. But she didn't care to face Mom yet either. She didn't know where she wanted to be. There wasn't any place to just get away from things for a while.

Maybe downtown? Easy enough to lose yourself in the hustle-bustle crowd jamming the sidewalks. Too hot outside to be walking very far, but town was only a few blocks. She could take a city bus home when she was ready to go. The idea of sitting among a bunch of sweaty faceless riders appealed to her.

The clomping of her shoes sounded louder than ever as she strode off down the sidewalk. She looked around to see if anyone was watching her and tried to make the shoes clatter less. The closer she got to the town center, the more her noise mingled with the whirr and squeal and rumble of the traffic and the shuffle of fellow walkers' shoes on the sidewalk. In spite of the sun beating down on her, she quickened her pace.

Bigger than life against a plate-glass window, a picture-perfect double-dip Baskin-Robbins ice cream cone invited her inside the parlor. A scoop of chocolate mint would be out of this world. Her saliva glands started pumping. She could sure use some pampering, and if she didn't do it, who would? And boy would it feel good just to get in out of this heat.

"What can I get for you today, miss?"

"Chocolate mint. In a sugar cone."

"Two dips today?"

"Nah." Hey, wait. Why not? "Sure. Make it two. Chocolate mint on bottom and rainbow sherbet on top."

The attendant had obviously never heard of such a wild combination. "Whatever you say," he said, with a shrug.

Kim felt a stir of adventure getting into her bones. Nibbling at the sweet coldness, she gazed out over the top of her cone through the plate glass to where the anxious swarm of beings plunged intensely forward along the sidewalk. A few moments before, she'd been part of the swarm, hustling just as blindly ahead to no purpose.

On they went—hard-faced middle-aged men in crisp business suits, tired-looking motherly women with teased hair and baggy slacks, adolescent boys, high-school dropouts with time to kill, in low-slung Levis and smoke haloing their heads, a few girls with blossoms embroidered on their blouse collars—all marching in step like an army on the move, their eyes dull and fixed or wandering idly about them, moving steadily onward to meet their fate. What did any of them know or care about somebody named Kim who'd just lost a stupid election? And what did *she* care about *them*?

She took tiny bites of her ice cream, making it last. The longer she watched the sidewalk army, the more apart from them she seemed, and the more she could feel her sense of humor returning. They really were simply absurd, tramping along like that, marching as to war. And not a smile among them. They didn't realize what a big joke it all was. The only way to stand it was to laugh at it. If you didn't laugh, the joke was on you.

They didn't deserve her sympathy, but she couldn't help feeling sorry for them anyway, taking things so very seriously. She wiped a tear—amusement or pity, she didn't know which—from her cheek and popped the last of her sugar cone into her mouth. It didn't taste very sweet.

She had to force herself out of the coolness of the ice-cream parlor into the heat and hassle of the sidewalk. Back in the flow, she found herself propelled along like a piece of driftwood. Her eye picked out the garish window of the Odds and Ends Shoppe. Their stuff was always fun to look at, such a fantastic mix of weird and showy, daring and tacky. That poster of a flying pig, what did it mean? Or those stuffed satin hearts, what were you supposed to make of them? They might be peculiar, but they were mysterious. They weren't everyone's bag. You had to work a little to like them.

But what on earth was that ungodly thing dangling like a splotchy snake on the wall? Could it really be a variegated patent-leather belt? It was certainly trying hard to camouflage itself. She had to look closer.

The clerk seemed surprised by her interest. "That sassy bit?" she said with a smile that humored Kim. "Oh it's going to take the right person to try that on!'

It had been marked down more than once, Kim saw. It would take guts to wear, the lady was right about that. Kim took it from its hook, wiped the dust off and wrapped it round her waist. A perfect fit, of course. All its oddness blended right in with the rest of her clothes. She and the belt were meant for each other, Kim thought, grinning at herself in the full-length mirror. And so cheap! Having eccentric tastes paid off sometimes.

She clattered out of the boutique holding her geometry book up against her chest to show off the spectacle twined round her waist. Hey, everyone! she wanted to shout, look here what I'm wearing! What do you say—too much, huh? Wake up, folks, Kim's back in town!

A woman with mail-order features was coming along the sidewalk toward her. Deliberately Kim stepped into her path. The woman stopped, clutching her handbag to her, and frowned. Her glance fell from Kim's eyes to the new belt. Her frown deepened. With a humph she made her way brusquely past Kim, muttering her disapproval in words Kim couldn't make out, and mingled back into the flow of the crowd.

Kim was delighted with the reaction she'd provoked. She'd given the woman a little test, and the woman had passed like a flying pig. Or was it the belt that had passed? Or was it Kim? It felt so good to be loose again. Maybe she ought to have her name embossed on the belt. She'd wear it to school tomorrow for Mr. Smith to gawk at and shake his head about.

Waiting for the 37th Street bus, Kim leaned against a phone booth, smiling at the memory of that woman's look of scorn.

• eight •

EXPOSITION

AT LAST THE BEGINNING

You've seen B through a key crisis and its consequences—that is, the *during* and *after* phases of the action—and are finally ready to look back to pre-crisis events, the *before* phase. This opening third of your story is the foundation everything else must stand on. If it is strong, it will support a strong crisis and resolution. If it is weak, the story will collapse no matter how good your Narratives C and D are. Because it fills in background that shows where your character B is coming from, it is usually called Exposition. So we'll label it Narrative E.

But if the idea of starting your story with something called "exposition" sounds so dull you feel like yawning, then by all means don't call it exposition. Call it the "opening" or "beginning" or "introductory" phase. Whatever you call it, its purpose is to lead your readers from the world outside into the world of your imagination. Functionally, that purpose is an explanatory one—preparing the ground your characters will walk, laying down the ground-rules they'll walk by, readying your readers to follow where they walk. Even if you end up deciding to start your story *in medias res* [in the middle of things], feeding in foreground data as needed by means of "flashback" (see below), your opening will still have to address the question of how to explain to readers joining your account in progress just what the state of affairs is.

If it's so important, and especially since it's the opening scene, why not write it first and let the rest of the story flow out of it? For at least two good reasons. One, hindsight is always clearer than foresight, so that you can do a better job of preparing the groundwork for events if you already know what they're going to be. And two, it's easier to concentrate your attention exclusively on the serious business of getting the stage set for the Big Event if your mind isn't always straining at the leash, eager to rush ahead to the yet-to-be-written crisis fireworks.

Does this mean that writing exposition is dull work, something to be put off till all the interesting stuff is finished, then done only because it has to be? Not at all. There is no reason why exposition should be less exciting to write—*or less interesting to read*—than any other phase of the story. Writing isn't good or bad because of its function, but because of how well it does its job. If it performs well, it's going to be interesting. The unbreakable rule in storytelling, as it is in other forms of writing, is to give readers what they need when they need it. And what they need to start off with is orientation, getting their bearings. It's a little like learning a new game. Best to go over the rules *beforehand* rather than start play knowing nothing and be told them only as the need arises. Most readers don't want to be baffled by a rush of events they haven't been given the necessary background to understand. Far from resenting your spending time to put them in the picture before the story's "main" event starts to unfold, they will appreciate your consideration.

One reason some beginning writers think exposition has to be boring is that they think it's always *un*dramatic. In the past, story openings often seemed burdened with elaborate descriptions of settings and everyone's physical appearance, with biographical data on all the central characters and a full-scale psychological work-up on the hero, all done in plain, direct, commentary prose. Nowadays, though, readers and writers alike seem to agree that needed exposition should be worked in without giving up all the excitement of plot development. Look at

Hemingway's dramatized opening scenes in "The Killers" or "Hills Like White Elephants." Recall the lively opening of Doud's "The Reasonable Request." And modern or not, Chekhov's "Turmoil" has a superbly efficient exposition.

This doesn't mean that serious writers resort to cheap narrative tricks to hook readers. "A shot rang out, shattering the intense stillness of the starless night, and with a piercing shriek the woman clutched her side and fell senseless to the floor" actually gives us less to get interested in than, say, "Puffing his cheeks in nervous rage, the stocky little man looked at his watch, jerked his briefcase from the cluttered desk and bustled out the door." The former, in one or another variation, is the epitome of the "grabber" opening used in conventional formula thrillers. The latter, at least partly because of its exposition, is more intriguing, hence more truly dramatic and so more likely to engage a reader's interest than a host of bodies dropping dead in the dark.

WHAT THE OPENING MUST ACCOMPLISH

The secret of writing a good beginning is to treat it with the very greatest respect. Always remember, it's not something that happens *before* the story starts; it *is* the start of the story, when readers are forming their first impressions and making up their minds about reading on. Just as with a game of chess, if you play your first ten moves badly, no amount of middle- or end-game savvy will stave off defeat.

However you go about motivating yourself, you'll need all your best skill to handle the diverse challenges these opening pages will offer. As already mentioned, the story's pre-crisis phase must give readers what they need to know about the main character in order to understand this person who is about to be subjected to stress. But it must do much more than introduce background information to get your story properly launched. It has to create the setting in which the action takes place, and not just the physical aspects but the feel of the location as well, what used to be called "atmosphere." It must establish the tone of your presentation, the "voice" it will be told in, so that readers can put themselves in the right mood—cheerful, gloomy, whimsical, whatever. It must pose your main character's central problem, so as to set a target for the plot to aim at. Finally, it must raise the thematic issue your story will deal with, and in a way that doesn't call attention to itself. Considering all you have to do, the problem with exposition isn't how to make it last long enough but how to pack it all in.

Another useful way to view the function of the opening is as an encounter between yourself as missionary and a tribe totally ignorant of your gospel. They are a tribe acquainted with the normal activities of everyday life, so that you needn't spend time explaining what houses or traffic or taxes are. But they know nothing of the people of your story, their personalities and problems. So for such particulars, you'll have to start from scratch, take nothing for granted. They also know nothing of you, either, so you'll need to establish your own credibility as well. Of course, as discussed in an earlier chapter, you have a certain built-in credibility just by being an author: fiction readers do want to trust fiction writers. But you must conduct yourself in a way to hold that trust. Taking this view of your responsibilities in the opening pages should keep you from making very many false assumptions or neglecting to make needed clarifications.

BACKWARDS IN TIME

So much for what, in general terms, the opening has to do. That still leaves you with the practical procedural question: What steps do I follow and in what order? First, get yourself back inside B's head and at a point in time shortly *after* the concluding scene just completed. Now, as B, cast your mind back over the past few days (no more than a week) and think about how your outlook on life has changed as a result of the crisis you've been through. In particular, think back to an exact day and hour before the storm hit, when life seemed truly different from what it does now—a time of which you're tempted to say, "What I *didn't* know then!" But it must also be a time—and this is essential—when you *could* have known, because the storm clouds of the upcoming tempest were on the horizon, if only you'd been clear-sighted enough to pick them out. It should feel a little like standing on a spot of high ground and looking back across a gulch you've just hiked through to that other high point on the far side that you started down from.

The main business of the exposition is to show B's outlook *before* the Core, so that readers can compare it with B's outlook *after* the Core (Narrative D). This means Narrative E must depict that same set of personal characteristics you focused on in Narratives C and D. Just as D gives the extent of the bend in B's attitude, E draws the straight and narrow path B would have traveled along had the crisis not occurred. Thus Narrative E completes the structural triangle which gives your story much of its stability. Once its exposition is done, your story is structurally complete—comparable to the diagram in Chapter 1 of a finished story's component phases. If we adapt that diagram to the terminology applied during your story's composition, we get the following graphic:

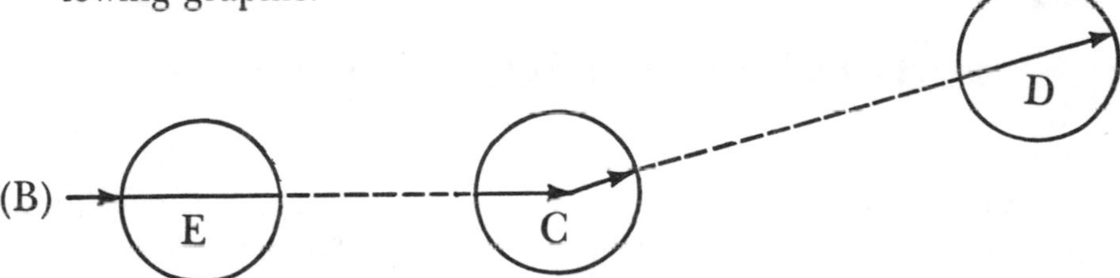

As with the other scenes you've done, Narrative E's time span ought to be limited to an hour or less. But unlike C and D, it is possible to widen the time-scope of your exposition by embedding bits of past times in it without damaging—even at times clarifying—its time-focus. In fiction-writing jargon this practice is called time-shifting, or more popularly "flashback." The use of time-shifting in fiction, like that of symbolism, has often been discussed in such a way as to exaggerate its difficulties. Actually it is as natural as memory. Something in the present causes us to recall something from the past that in turn triggers a sequential recollection which actually takes over our conscious attention and so interrupts our awareness of present time. In the same way flashbacks may interrupt B's flow of present-time awareness with pieces from the past, which take over the story's time flow for the duration of B's concentration on them.

You may find time-shifting a helpful tool when trying to

squeeze in all the exposition your story needs into so short a segment of "elapsed present" time. Several scenes from various times can be gathered with a single backward reach, all while only a few minutes actually pass. But though flashbacks are just as natural as symbolism, they are not as inevitable. Symbols will creep in, like them or not, but time shifts won't happen unless you choose to introduce them. And you shouldn't try using them anwhere but in Narrative E. Why? Because flashback, as its name implies, is all about filling in the present with the past, and you should do all your filling in *before* the story enters its crisis scene. Exposition prepares for what's to come; it doesn't make excuses for what's already happened. So there's no more place for flashbacks in the crisis or conclusion than for the inept joke teller's "I should have told you" or "I forgot to mention" just before his punch line.

FORESHADOWING AND SUSPENSE

If you could see into the future, you could rule the world. Knowing the future of your story, you can lay out today's history with an uncanny sense of tomorrow's events. To seed exposition with corn that looks ordinary enough but comes up armed men in the next scene is known as foreshadowing. It is an ancient technique, used masterfully by Greek dramatists to set up tragically ironic conclusions. But its power can be abused. When Mary Roberts Rinehart injected herself into a tale of mystery and intrigue to remark, "Had she but known . . .," she went too far. Any time a writer calls his readers' attention to the fact that he sees the future, he has gone too far. Chekhov's famous dictum should be the rule of foreshadowing: If a gun is noticed hanging on the wall in the opening scene, it must be fired before the story ends. The gun need not radiate significance when it is introduced. That it has been singled out for notice will tell readers to remember it.

The chief effect of foreshadowing is suspense. As clues to the unfolding mystery accumulate (every story is some sort of mystery), readers find more and more to wonder and worry about. Who will use that gun on the wall? How? When? On whom? With what results? Suspense arises from the reader's concern about an unknown future. But the writer knows that future and so can make sure that the only questions raised are ones the story will answer. This is what proper exposition, legitimate foreshadowing, and genuine suspense are all about. They are promises made to readers to repay their investment of aroused curiosity with satisfactory, substantial answers.

Failing to live up to this implicit understanding is a breach of the Fiction Contract and brings the good name of story writing into disrepute. So don't mislead readers with red herrings. Don't promise more than you intend to deliver. The great Dickens himself was guilty of dropping clues almost at random in the early chapters of his novels. His excuse (in case he needs one) is that his novels were being printed in monthly parts just as fast as he could improvise them, and he wanted to be sure he'd given himself plenty of leads to choose what to follow up from. If he'd had the leisure to write his novels wholly in advance of their publication, he might have made a tidier job of them. The point being that the errors of genius are no more worth imitating than any other errors.

Properly handled, suspense does not lead to surprise. A surprise ending, by definition, is one that takes readers off guard, unprepared. The kind of ending you've written (if you did it by *The Primer*) is one that grows naturally and logically from the Core. It is grounded in and justified by the Exposition you're about to compose. Contrary to what you may have supposed when you sat down to write your story, a surprise ending is usually a failed ending. A hundred years ago, the tales of O. Henry were admired for their trick endings. A poor man sells his watch to buy his wife some hair combs for Christmas, and surprise! she's sold her hair to buy him a watch fob. Or a bedfast invalid declares she'll die when the last leaf falls from a vine outside her window, but miraculously that last leaf clings stubbornly on and the invalid, taking it as a sign, regains her will to live. Surprise: that last leaf was actually hand-painted by an aging artist whose heroics brought about his death from exposure.

Such snappy finishes are no longer greatly respected or often imitated. The answers they provide to the questions they raise are simply inadequate. Today's readers don't seem to crave syrup-sweet sentimentality. They want an honest look at the way real people cope with actual problems. The developments of O. Henry's "The Gift of the Magi" and "The Last Leaf" are so phony, the behavior of their characters so utterly unbelievable, that the author cannot even trust the situation to make its own impact but must step in himself to plead, against reason, for the moralistic messages these stories were supposed to illustrate. Yet another "lesson from a master" in how *not* to do it!

If you have planned and executed Narratives C and D by the book, your readers should have a sense of how in general your story is going to turn out, paragraphs or even pages before it actually ends. Meaning, your conclusion is "predictable." But only in the way *Hamlet* or the *Egmont* Overture is. This kind of predictability isn't a fault; it's a strength, and it's called inevitability. What it means is that the story resolves responsibly, in the direction it was headed, rather than slinking or dodging about trying to avoid the obvious exit. An inevitable ending is a satisfying one because it fulfills your readers' expectations of what *should* happen.

If you regard your opening as a time for making promises to be kept, defining a problem to be solved, stating a proposition to be proved, you won't be likely to let readers down. That way, rather than thinking in terms of pulling the wool over the eyes of your trusting audience with tricky misdirection or disinformation (which they'll swallow, remember, especially early on), you'll be playing fair and trying honestly to find the right answer to the question the story asks. Besides, any whoppers you tell to hook your audience's attention at first will only come back to haunt you in the end when readers find they've been swindled. Why borrow trouble?

MAKING THE OPENING PHASE APPEAR

Chances are that by now you've got a fairly clear picture of your Narrative E in your mind's eye. Often, once Narratives C and D are in place, E seems to emerge almost of its own accord, without your having to give much conscious thought to it. The father/son story idea we ran through back in chapter 6 involved an argument that happened partly because of Dad's bad day at the office. "Boss" automatically became an important motivating factor, causing Dad to drive to his house after the row. The opening scene of this story almost has to be the one between Dad and Boss at work.

But what if, after all your reminiscing about B's past few days, no beginning episode has revealed itself to you? What can you do to make the necessary event materialize for you? First of all, remind yourself of what the beginning must accomplish. It has to present B in such a way as to engage reader interest in and respect for both B's character and the challenges B is to face. It has to show us the personal qualities that will sustain B during the crisis and the defects that will be exposed by it—B's "Achilles heel." It should be dramatic enough to give readers something to watch, but not so dramatic as the Core; E's job is to prepare for C, not steal its thunder. And it must manage to work in those questions of plot and theme that stir reader curiosity. If necessity is really the mother of invention, such a list of needs should goad your imagination into action.

But say you've raised all these leading questions with yourself and you still haven't been led anywhere. In such case, you'll have to resort to more vigorous forcing of the issue. Study the structural and thematic lines of your Denouement, Narrative D. Look at it as the down-ramp from your Core, thinking of E as the up-ramp. What you want from your opening scene is an "idea-shape" to balance against the ending, a rising action to balance its falling action, a reverse reflection of its pattern. Symbolically, the opening should contain images that are echoed and resonated in the conclusion. The mood and tone, likewise, ought to be charged with certain similarities. Such resemblances can help point up the essential differences in your character's status.

Don't worry much about plot particulars at this point, other than to keep things pointing generally in the direction of the Core's showdown. Instead, concentrate on setting and atmosphere—potential "environmental" parallels between the scene you've just finished (D) and the one to be written. If you still can't decide just where or how to begin, take some bit of physical detail from your conclusion that has (or ought to have) a symbolic edge to it and use it to get your first sentence going.

This may seem arbitrary, but the fact is that it's as good a way to start as any other, and better than most. You don't want to get hung up on some mystical search for "just the right" opening sentence. The success of your story doesn't depend on the perfection of any sentence, first, second, or thousandth. It depends on the soundness and significance of your coverage, paragraph after paragraph, of a crisis in B's life. Good sentences are important, just as the quality of bricks in a wall is important, but never forget that it's the overall story rather than the sentences, the wall and not the individual bricks, that really counts.

The student author of our ongoing sample was one of those who got stuck for an opening scene. In the end she had to resort to the kind of scene-forcing just described. (The telephone in the first sentence was cued by the phone booth in the last one.) Knowing this, see how much evidence of arbitrary data selection, deliberate drawing of parallels between the opening and closing scenes, you can find. How well does the student succeed in making this synthesized action seem as real as that in the Core, which we know was based on actual experience? Are the symbolic links between episodes strong enough to help bind the story together, yet inconspicuous enough not to call attention to themselves? (Note that the usual two-stage process of composition—preparing a single-page summary "plan" and then expanding it to three pages—has been simplified to "all in one go." If you'd rather do a short sketch first, then spread it out, feel free to do so.)

Sample Narrative E

Kim picked up the receiver and dialed Linda's number. Before it could ring, she hung up. What could she have to say to Linda at 8:00 a.m. that wouldn't wait for an hour? Wish her luck? Linda didn't need luck. Just long enough coat tails to take Kim in with her. Together, they'd make Council hum. With all Kim's ideas and Linda's way of getting things done, they'd revolutionize Central.

"Mom?" Kim called, not really expecting an answer. She had usually gone to work by eight. Kim lifted the receiver again and dialed Donna's number. "Donna? Kim. No need to come past for me today. I feel like walking. See you at school."

Only she didn't feel like walking. She felt like, well, running. Away from it all. At least till today was over. Then maybe she could look people in the face again. Funny, after all that campaigning, to still feel like a stranger at Central. She just couldn't blend in.

She clomped off down the sidewalk in her wooden shoes. Going to be another hot one. She could feel herself starting to sweat already. Stupid to be walking two miles when she could have ridden. She kicked at the grass forcing its way between the cracks in the sidewalk. It got stepped on all day, but never stamped out. Somehow it always came back. Ought to kill it with salt so it'd quit splitting the walks.

Somebody ought to fix up old Central High too, she thought, trudging up the steps. She felt old and tired herself. It's going to take more than Student Council to spruce up this dump and its worn-out ways. It tolerated her all right, but that wasn't the same as approving of her. How could she be an outsider at Central, when she and her Mom had been in this same stupid town as long as she could remember. Why did everyone in Topeka have to think every last boring thing about Topeka was the biggest deal on earth? Topeka wasn't exactly the center of the universe.

There was Steve Sanderson, big-dog Steve, sitting cool in the sun, leaned back against the old brown brick wall, looking off into space to give everyone a good look at him. Kim did look, wishing he'd turn and look at her the way he had last August. "Hi, Blondie!" She could still hear him: "You new here?" But going blond hadn't made any lasting difference. He never smiled at her anymore, never started conversations. Linda said she'd scared him. Kim pressed her lips together. She could have used a smile today.

She pushed the heavy wood door open. It swung back at her, nicking the tip of her bare big toe. She could have screamed from the pain, but she only clenched her teeth and muttered about ten quick damns.

Inside, artistically posed in an archway, Jennifer studied her fingernails. Ought to be outside with Steve having an ignoring contest. Jenny'd win, of course, she had so much class she couldn't even smile because it disturbed her high fashion image. Probably crack her make-up too, Kim thought with a smirk. Jenny brushed a hand delicately over her ebony hair, which was pulled up in a chignon. A big gold class ring with a topaz stone in it shone on one finger. Probably Jim's ring, maybe Randy's. Hard to know with

Jennifer. Kim could never figure why she went for the creeps she did, but then Jennifer wasn't there to be understood, just admired.

"Hi Jenny," Kim said, beaming her election smile.

"Oh hi, Kim. How's it?" Jennifer blinked slowly.

"OK, I guess. Maybe a little nervous."

"Oh yeah? What's to be nervous about?"

"Jennifer! You haven't forgot Council elections?"

"Oh that. You running?"

You never knew with Jennifer just how much her lack of awareness was put on to impress you with her indifference to ordinary events. "You know I am," Kim said. "You're voting, aren't you?"

"If I do," Jennifer drawled, "I'll look for your name. But don't count on it." The outermost corners of her lips lifted in a thin smile. "You can't really care about anything so trivial, can you?"

Could she? Kim wondered, knowing Jennifer was the last person in the world to be interested in the answer to the question. "Thanks, Jenny. Seen Linda?"

Jennifer rolled her eyes. "Did I! Hideous red, just asking Central's bulls to gore her."

Jenny, jealous of Linda? Kim didn't have time to work that one out. She needed to find Linda and get herself pumped up again. Linda had got her into this in the first place and now she'd have to get her through it. Kim saw the bright red sun dress down the hall, and yelled "Linda!" Her voice echoing back and forth between the gray metal lockers sounded pinched and hollow. As she approached, she could see Linda's bright dark eyes dancing with excitement.

"Hey, Kim, Kim, Vigor and Vim!" Linda chanted, the words of Kim's campaign slogan filled with energy. All Kim's confidence came back in a rush. If Linda believed in what they were doing, Kim knew it would come out O.K.

Hands clasped, they went to their lockers. Side by side they worked at their combinations. Linda opened her door, but Kim was having trouble. "Damn this lock," she said, "it won't work for me."

Sally sauntered up, long blond hair over one shoulder, hands shoved deep in the pockets of baggy jeans. She swung a hip playfully into Kim. "Whoa, kid, you're going to break something."

"Why does my lock have to be tougher than anyone else's?" Kim raged, knowing it wasn't true but too mad to care.

"It's as tough as you make it, kid," Sally said.

Kim felt like smacking the fat grin off Sally's big lips. "Quit calling me kid," she said.

"Only kidding," Sally said, backing off.

Linda had Kim's locker open. She always remembered things like birthdays, first names, and other people's locker combinations. "There you go, buddy."

"Thanks."

Sally winced at the mound of debris in the bottom of Kim's locker. "Wow, old banana skins!" Sally couldn't resist a good tease. "Odor of orange peel maybe, but rotten banana skins? What you saving *them* for?" She let out a high-pitched, good-natured cackle, and Kim couldn't stay mad at her. How come Sally could get away with it, when every time Kim tried kidding people they got mad?

"Sally," Linda asked, "you ready for elections?" Sally was another of Linda's recruits. Kim couldn't see what Linda saw in her or why she thought Sally would be good for Council.

"Should I have dressed up?" Sally asked in mock-seriousness, and she and Linda laughed.

Kim was sure Sally didn't care enough. She slammed her locker door shut with a bang.

• nine •

INTEGRATION

A PAUSE TO REFRESH

Your first assignment in this chapter should be the easiest to follow you've ever been given—unless you're a chronic worrier or a workaholic. Ignore your story as completely as you can for as long as you can: two days, two weeks, two months if you can. Of course if you're working to somebody else's deadline, you won't be able to decide for yourself how much "neglect time" to take. But if you can set your own pace and aren't in a big rush, I'd urge ripening a fresh manuscript in cold storage for about half a year. That's likely to be time enough for it to escape from your close-in sensitivity range, but not so long as to lose your concern for its people or issues. And don't just keep from looking at the manuscript. Actually forget about it completely. Distract yourself with other projects. Build something. Go fishing. Start another story if you have to. Keep your mind off this one.

But if you quit thinking about it, won't you lose all that specialized knowledge of its inner workings you've acquired during the long hours of putting it together? That's what you'd like to happen, but unfortunately you'll have to make do with losing only some of it. At this stage your biggest obstacle to effective re vision is knowing too much, not too little, about your story. The process of writing a story inevitably engenders a feeling of closeness between you and your work. It has often been likened to the bond between parent and child. Just as parents find it hard to see flaws in their offspring, artists have difficulty spotting defects in their artifacts. Knowing all the work you've put into it, you are likely to be so impressed with your story's strengths that you overlook its weaknesses.

Ideally you'd like to look at your completed rough draft as if someone else had written it. You need to stand back and appraise it objectively, like a would-be home buyer making a skeptical inspection of a house for sale, rather than as the architect, builder, or realtor trying to sell it. The closer you can come to the stance of unbiased outsider with no prior experience of the story, the more likely you are to see how it can be improved. You can't reasonably hope for total objectivity about something that involves you so personally, but in the same way as time heals wounds it will gradually lower your feeling of identification with the story's situation and allow you to admit that for all its merit it's not yet perfect and might possibly be altered for the better.

As a test of your "sensitivity level" ask yourself how you feel about having someone else read and comment on your story. If you find that the idea makes you uncomfortable, you probably aren't detached enough from your work yet to look at it critically. If you think it wouldn't bother you to have another person take a look, and know of someone who won't just tell you how wonderful it is, by all means request the reading. Then keep a finger on your pulse when your reader starts pointing out possible deficiencies to see whether you can stay cool under fire. If you can listen calmly to criticism of your story without taking it as any sort of personal attack on your talent, intelligence, or values, you are in a proper frame of mind to begin final revision.

END OF THE HOLIDAY

Having had your "cooling off" period, you must now settle down to the task of fine-tuning your story's machinery and giving it a finishing stylistic polish. This is another potentially dangerous time for story writers. It can be hard, after a period of separation from your work, to recover your zest for it—one reason why there are so many "almost done" stories gathering dust in desk drawers. Even experienced writers have to struggle against the "post-partum depression" that normally follows the completion of a story's first draft, the feeling that the real work's done and it's time to relax. To let down just now, before doing the final draft, is to depreciate the value of all you've invested in the story so far. Treating final-drafting casually or with indifference is saying in effect that you don't really care if your finished story fits together properly or flows smoothly, and taking a "like me, like my fleas" attitude toward readers—not at all engaging.

Another malaise that sometimes attacks writers at this stage of the composition process is "finishing phobia," a form of perfectionism that can keep publishable material from ever getting out of its author's hands. Also called "page fright," this fear that one's work is imperfect, and therefore unfit for public exhibition, must be met and overcome. It sometimes helps to remind yourself that twinges of inadequacy and feelings of self-doubt are normal and nearly universal, and that the capacity for self-criticism is essential to the job of revision you are about to undertake. But then go on to tell yourself as well that you're not going to allow any phony humility to keep you from completing your story and letting the world have a look at it. How many of the authors of the "perfect" stories you've read were fully satisfied with them as they were submitted for publication? Believe me, none. The "perfect" draft, like tomorrow, never arrives. We must learn to do our work of story-building thoroughly, including the fine-tuning and final polishing, then respect what we've done enough to put it from the nest and see if it can fly on its own.

So, however you accomplish it, your first post-vacation job is to square yourself for the demanding but rewarding final phase of your story's progress toward a finished final draft. Now, supposing you're all pumped up and ready to go, get out your manuscript and make sure it's all in order: Narrative E, followed by C, followed by D—approximately nine pages of sequenced narrative relating a single developing series of events in three distinct phases separated by two time gaps. The text, whether handwritten or typed, should be neat and clean enough to be read easily without distracting detours to include insertions (marginal or interlinear) or to skip big blocks of X'd-out material. Find a marker of distinctive color (one you won't confuse with others already in use in the manuscript), and sit back prepared to enjoy a good story—supposing yours turns out to be one.

For this first screening, pretend you're a reader who's mainly concerned with being able to follow the action. Without stopping to figure out why it occurs, just note in the margin whenever the smooth forward movement of the story's action seems to falter. Pay special attention to those points where the focus changes—from exterior events to interior perceptions, from one time or place to another (as in the gaps between segments). Remember, your sole purpose this time through is to spot breaks in the narrative chain. The most basic weakness of all, it's the first one you need to attend to. If readers can't track you from one sentence to the next, they won't stick with your story long.

Once you've tagged all the instances of coherence breakdown or transition failure, you should mend the bad patches one way or another. It is not possible here to make a list of all the kinds of narrative incoherence and the remedies for them. The nature of the problem is invariably the same: a segment in the sequence is missing. The solution is obviously to supply the missing segment and so bridge the gap.

Second reading, pretend you're a movie director planning to film the story and need to decide on camera angles, especially when to switch from one perspective to another. In fiction, it's usual to begin a new paragraph when a change in viewing angle would occur. (The logic of fiction paragraphing is so different from ordinary paragraphing logic that indenting in a story probably ought to be called "narragraphing" just to distinguish it from the normal paragraph formatting.) Thus, customarily in passages of dialog every change of speaker brings a new paragraph as the camera's eye moves to watch each participant in turn.

Sometimes, even if no break in the coverage comes to signal a new paragraph, the narrative may seem to want a breather, in the way a film scene requires relief from a single sustained angle or distance. A subtle shift in tone may need a slight pause for readers to make an attitude adjustment. Occasionally an author will start a new paragraph strictly for dramatic effect. Of course this should be done very sparingly. Like exclamation points, the emphasis of miniparagraphs is lost by frequent use.

Narragraphing may also help you solve some of the coherence problems tagged in your first screening. Indenting asks the reader to pause for a short leap forward, which can be as good as a bridge. So rather than composing two or three sentences linking two narrative segments, try the effect of simply starting a new paragraph. If your readers can make the leap easily, you and they are both better off without the deadwood of "transition" sentences. If the gap is too large to bridge with simple indenting, you may still be able to span it with the "super paragraph"—an extra band of white space across the page which draws a very conspicuous line between two masses of text. (In ordinary double-spaced typescript, you leave three lines blank.) Large time lapses between story phases are prime candidates for such indicated breaks. Caution: Don't assume *all* gaps can be managed by skillful narragraphing. Only if a connection between two text masses is already implicit in them *as written* can you expect readers to jump the discontinuity. Otherwise you must write the necessary bridging sentences.

Once you're satisfied that the paragraphing makes sense and does its job of guiding readers along the story's winding path, you should read over the sections of dialog. If you followed the advice in chapter 5, you voiced all your characters' speeches as you wrote them to make sure none were unspeakable. But now you need to give the whole story a vocal run-through. If you're working on your own, you'll have to do your best to imitate the speaking manner of each separate character and listen to yourself at the same time. If you can coax others into reciting your story to you, especially if they are able to catch the unique lilt of your various characters' voices, you'll get an even better feel for how well their speeches work.

Look both for "oral validity"—that is, whether the lines have the sound of actual human speech—and "psychological validity"—meaning whether what each character says is in line with his mental makeup at the time. Is each voice individualized? Consistent with itself? Again, there's no easy fix for unconvincing dialog. But having spotted it, don't give up fiddling with it till it satisfies both your ear and your sense of each character's unique outlook.

READ IT AGAIN, SAM

Having reinspected your story three times, you may be starting to feel you're back inside it again. But try to stay detached for at least one final reading. Don your logic-chopper's hat and prepare to run everything through your reasoning mill. You'll be looking for violations of three principles of rationality: conciseness, relevance, and consistency. Whether you can deal with all three in a single reading or will need to concentrate on each separately, be sure your screening is a thorough one.

CONCISENESS means saying what you have to say as efficiently as you can. It doesn't mean writing everything in a clipped, terse, telegraphic style. It means not wasting words. You can get away with squandering your own time, but if you try squandering your readers' time you'll quickly find yourself with no audience. Be like Coleridge's Ancient Mariner, stopping a wedding guest to tell your tale: to keep him from attending to his other business you need to be as near spellbinding as possible. Long words and long sentences should be seen as possibly compressible. Of course sometimes they are the most precise means of expression available, but even then they can be inefficient if they muddle the reader's head. Look closely at any repetition of words or ideas. It may be needed for emphasis, but it may be pure redundancy, in which case it should go. Every wasted word lowers the energy of its sentence. Every wasted sentence drains the power of its paragraph. A wasted paragraph saps the strength of the whole story. Padding of any sort is a dangerous softness: it makes readers doze off when they're supposed to be driving. So if you write, "The little three-year-old child's tiny hands were encased in small woolen mittens that were dark blue in color," when "The toddler wore navy blue mittens" would serve you just as well, you're guilty of wordiness.

RELEVANCE, as you know, means that every detail must contribute to the story's central purpose. Wordiness is itself a species of verbal irrelevance, but even after you've pruned the deadwood out, your concise sentence may still not be of use. The fact that the toddler wore navy blue mittens may simply not matter. Out of context, the statement's utility can't really be measured. But to be relevant, *all* its data must count: the child itself, its approximate age, the mittens, and the mittens' color. And it's no good saying the child needs mittens because it's winter. In that case the child may also need thermal underwear and earmuffs, which only raises another question: Why does it have to be so cold?

If coldness is necessary to the story's meaning, and the mittens help establish that sense of coldness, then mittens may well be relevant. But do they need to be blue? Not if your only excuse is that it's the color Mom picked out or, even worse, that you just happened to think blue. You and real-life Moms are free to follow whims in the ordinary world, but in the extraordinary world of fiction nothing goes for nothing. Maybe blue means something in the story's color code (it could help suggest either the innocence of the child or the indifference of the mother, for instance) or maybe it intensifies the chill of the story's atmosphere or serves the story's purpose in some other useful way. The point: it has to be of some use, and you as author ought to know what that use is.

CONSISTENCY is integrity of presentation. Readers must feel that they know your main character as an actual personality with an identifiable presence, as "solid" in all but physical body as anyone they know in the real world. Much of this solidity comes from the character's behavioral consistency. We recognize people because they act the way we expect them to. When they don't, we say "You're not yourself today."

Of course stories aren't about the ordinary days in people's lives, so the actions of fictional characters can't be ordinary either. But for such invented persons to seem real, they must have some more or less normal self to deviate from when their lives turn exceptional. Whatever your fictional characters get up to, they should always stay within their probability limits. When they surprise, they must surprise in a convincing way, so that the reader's dubious "Oh no" quickly changes to a positive "Oh yes!" of acceptance. Now's the time to make sure your main character's bedrock personality—the sum of all those index qualities you've been calling attention to—is solid and steady enough to give it a recognizable consistency.

The consistency of your characters' behavior depends on the steadiness with which you portray them. Your puppets dance to the tune you play, so that you can kill their integrity by simply playing the wrong tune. Adopt a mocking tone in your authorial commentary and no amount of earnestness on their part can stand against it. An essential part of consistency is thus the compatibility of your story's subject matter and your manner in telling it. One reason the bloody conclusion of Flannery O'Connor's "A Good Man Is Hard to Find" troubles some readers is that it seems unfair, given the jaunty tone of the story's first half. O'Connor may have bent the rules and got away with it, but it's not an example to be followed.

Yet another kind of consistency to check out is your "unity of perspective." Every moment of every scene shown must be observed and reported from the vantage point of your character B. The story is a history of B's impressions, and no one else's can be allowed to enter into it except as they enter through B's awareness. To be sure, B is only acting out your ideas and speaking your words. But the illusion must be maintained that B is speaking and acting free from any manipulation. Be sure that your guiding hand is at no point visible to the audience.

Finally, while you still have your logician's hat on, take a look at your network of symbols. To be effective, a symbol normally recurs here and there throughout the story, so as to "burn in" its code. Your Core, in particular, may be suffering from some symbolic sag, since it was composed before you were consciously and actively working up symbolic potential. This is also a good time to remedy any shortfall in concreteness you may have found when you were inspecting your manuscript for symbolic raw material back in chapter 7.

DOTTED I'S AND CROSSED T'S

It may seem too obvious to need saying, but you should give your manuscript a good old-fashioned English-teacherish going over for basic mechanical, grammatical, and syntactic errors, including "typewriter mistakes." Professional writers tend to be very fussy about ccc (clean correct copy). But beginners' manuscripts sometimes look as if their authors don't feel the need to obey the conventions of standard usage, as if they thought creativity were some lawless land where geniuses all spoke in gibberish. Don't kid yourself. Real artists are the preservers and protectors of their art's traditions, not anarchists bent on wrecking the system. It's for you and your fellow literates to guard the precious heritage of our language.

But even if you didn't have a duty to the language, you'd still have a duty to your readers and the story you're offering them. A story is a gift, and a gift should not be an insult. A story is also a message, and a message should not be garbled. Treat your readers with respect and they'll return the favor. Giving them foul rather than fair copy is treating them with contempt, and they'll know how to return that favor as well. But perhaps your greatest duty of all is to the story itself, abstract as that may sound. The quality of your workmanship is a measure of the value you place on your story.

No matter how big-time your plans may be, if your writing competence is bush-league, your story will be too. The age-old debate over the relative importance of concept and expression can't be settled because form *is* meaning and meaning *is* form. There's a great sculpture inside every block of marble, but till all the surrounding stone has been painstakingly chipped away it doesn't really exist. So if you're tempted to argue that your ideas are just too powerful for your sentences, better think again: your sentences *are* your ideas.

This doesn't mean that you will be hiding your unique stylistic flair in the drab conventional clothing of standard form. Writers have as great an obligation to make their individual voices heard as they do to keep up the traditions of good usage. Language is kept alive by its users always finding new resources in it. But real distinctiveness isn't going to be stifled by conventions any more than a colorful personality gets lost in a dress suit. If you have genius, don't worry about its showing: no amount of correctness can conceal it. You can afford to be mannerly.

Sticking to the rules of standard English should also not be seen as contradicting the advice about letting characters speak in a natural, colloquial way. You must of course be free to report the actual words your people utter, grammatical or not. Your point-of-view character, in particular, must be permitted to have his say unedited by you. If B is a poor grammarian, some of that roughness is bound to show, in his speech and in his thoughts as well. But his lapses should occur only at your bidding and with the story's best interests in mind.

A BOW FOR YOUR GIFT PACKAGE

By now you've done four or more rereadings and the rewritings needed to fix what you found wrong. Isn't it about time to call this project finished? Very nearly. But there's one vital bit of writing yet to do. In case you'd forgotten, your story still needs a title. Some writers, even experienced ones, feel a reluctance, almost a repugnance, to putting titles on their works. The reason for this is probably that authors tend to distrust labels, and calling a story one thing rather than another is to a degree restricting its meaning.

The title is also the one point in your story where you speak *as author* directly to readers rather than through your character. Proposing a title is thus a little like stepping in front of the curtain before a play's stage action begins to make an announcement, and it makes some writers nervous. Nevertheless, a title will be needed. No point saying you won't have one. You'll have to call your story something, and since a title like "Opus One" or "Untitled" is really more negative than neutral you may as well decide to make the best of it.

So what are the criteria for good titles? First of all, since it's the first thing your readers encounter, it probably ought to make them want to read on. It ought to LURE. On this basis, "The Pit and the Pendulum" is a better title than "William Wilson," and "The Beast in the Jungle" better than "Fordham Castle." Not to say that the latter titles aren't the right ones for their respective stories, only that they're far from catchy. Another useful quality in a title is an ironic edge, or BITE. By this yardstick, "The Tell-Tale Heart" is even a better title than "The Pit and the Pendulum." Both are intriguing, but whereas the latter adds no fresh insight for those familiar with the story, the former makes us shudder each time we compare its hint of romance (beforehand) with its grisly actual significance (afterward). A third criterion is accuracy. Your title ought to CAPTURE your story's central effect or purpose. "William Wilson" sounds like, and should be, a character study. If it is, then its title passes the accuracy test, even if it's not exactly seductive. Last, and least, a title is a HANDLE of sorts to pick your story up by, a name to call it. Normally, the easier the mouthful the better. "The Killers" is certainly a handier title than "The Short Happy Life of Francis Macomber," whatever compensating merits the latter may have.

If you can come up with an alluring, incisive, accurate handle for your story, you'll have put a fine bow on your package.

THE PLEASURE AND PAIN OF FEEDBACK

If you have been composing your story as a member of a writing group, you may already have felt the mixed emotions that go with letting others read and comment on your work. Getting "outside" criticism in one form or another is an important part of the crafting process. Other readers can really help you see your own work objectively. In order to keep from being influenced too much by any one critic, it's good to have many different readers rather than a select few.

Each approach to getting feedback has its pluses and minuses. Sharing your story with others piecemeal from the start can be scary, but it may be less awful than suddenly having to let somebody see "the whole thing" all at once. Whether others have read your work up to now or not, the time to hear what they can tell you has definitely arrived.

Even if you're not in a writing group you can probably locate a few literate humans to give your piece a quick read and tell you what they think. They don't have to be writers themselves, or even regular story readers, to make good critics. Even those who don't know a thing about art but do know what they like can sometimes be helpful. Don't be a snob about who can read your stuff. And don't be a coward either. Save your sensitivity for your writing, rather than wasting it fretting about whether people are going to be impressed. Chances are, no reader will give your work all the credit it deserves, but that's the worst even hostile readers can do to you. They can't eat you. They can't even destroy your story. They can only not like it, and you can live with that.

If you live alone on an island, or among total strangers, or are simply too pathologically shy to face an encounter with a reader of your work, you'll have to rely on the postal service. Pick a likely looking "little" magazine title from some sourcebook like *Writer's Market* or *Fiction Writer's Market* and send a ccc (clean correct copy) of your story off to its fiction editors, telling them you have only recently begun writing stories and would be grateful for their reactions to yours. Editors of such periodicals tend to sympathize with beginners and often take the time to send back fairly elaborate critiques in their willingness to help. The busier commercial giants, understandably, can't pay staff to comment on unaccepted submissions; they'll pay you for your stories once you've arrived, but they're not going to tell you how to get there.

Not all fiction editors—including those of lower-circulation literary journals—will provide feedback, but if you have the patience to send your story out to a number of different magazines (one after the other, not all at once) you will end up with a fair sample of opinion. However, it all hangs on your making the first move. No one can help you if you won't ask. Before performing any additional surgery on your patient, you need second, third, fourth opinions. Let neither false modesty nor false pride keep you from getting them. You're neither too bad nor too good for others to read.

Whoever ends up reading and criticizing your story, always bear in mind that their function is strictly advisory. All they can do is to tell you how the story affects them. However godlike their judgments may sound, they are only opinions, and those opinions aren't marching orders. The best criticism is that which shows it appreciates your intentions and points out specifically where the story falls short of achieving them. The worst sort of criticism is that which urges the critic's own fictional tastes (the "like this, don't like that" manner) and offers to collaborate with you by proposing material improvements to your story. The only catch is, even the best-intentioned critics can be wrong, and the most egocentric boor occasionally hits the bull's-eye, so you'll need to sift critical reaction to your work very carefully.

If you are receiving criticism face to face and so can interact with your critics, keep the ball in their court as much of the time as you can by repeatedly asking the world's best question, "Why?" Call their attention to areas of the story you are especially concerned about, but in a nondirective way—you want their impressions to be guided only by the story itself. And of course try to keep them from making collaborative comments. Most reader/critics respond positively to being reminded that what you need from them is their reactions, that the rethinking and rewriting of the story is your job. You may feel tempted to explain or defend your work, especially if your critics seem to have read something totally different from what you think you wrote, but self-justification is worse than pointless. If you try explaining to readers how you want them to read, you make it impossible for them to form an opinion of the story itself. You will have yourself become the troublesome collaborator interfering with what isn't your business, preempting any objective judgment of your story's evidence with an "insider" interpretation.

Remind yourself as you listen to criticism that its chief value lies in its externalness rather than its penetration. It gives you a line on how readers may react to your management of your fictional material. Whether fair or not, their reactions should help you decide what changes in strategy you need to make, if any. Unless you have reason to believe that a critic is hostile to you for some reason, and thus deliberately misreading your purpose, you should take seriously any mistaken impression your story seems to create, especially if it is one shared by several readers.

If you rely entirely on editorial criticism by mail, of course you simply take what you get, which is often not very comprehensive (or for that matter, comprehensible—and I speak as a practicing editor of over twenty years' experience!). In such a pass, you should probably send some copies of your provisional completed draft to various reader friends who won't mind your asking them a series of follow-up questions about it afterward.

YOUR FINAL DRAFT

Before you send up a last hurrah, this last sobering word about final revision: Sometimes it's better to *rewrite* than to *revise*—that is, to scrap whole sentences or even paragraphs and make a fresh go at a stretch of prose that no amount of tinkering seems able to fix. It is hard for writers to sacrifice sentences they have written. All writers naturally have a great affection for words, and most of us tend to become especially attached to our own as we string them together. Each time our eyes pass over one of our sentences, it's like stroking a pet cat. The more we pet it, the louder it purrs and the less we can think of parting with it. So we find ourselves with a whole houseful of darling pet squatters we can't bear to evict, which lie around taking up space, mewing for attention, and generally making a nuisance of themselves. As with those charming irrelevancies discussed in chapter 5, beginning writers are slightly more prone to this sort of infatuation simply because they've written fewer sentences, and so have more at stake in each of them. Once you've turned out your thousands and tossed away your hundreds, you begin to see them more as bricks, less as pets.

The point is, since sentences can be so lovely and distracting, you may be better off redoing certain parts of your story *without* reference to the original version. Oftentimes, if things sag or drag at some point for no clear reason, especially if the prose seems unusually fine, you should seriously consider rewriting the passage from scratch. Separating yourself from the words of the original will frequently unlock your view of what the story—apart from its language—really needs. If you persist in recasting such passages sentence by excruciating sentence, you may never discover the remedy for what ails them. They may be badly written simply because the idea they are striving to express is poorly conceived. At worst you'll end up with two unsuccessful versions. At best you'll be out of the woods. What usually happens is that the new version gets you enough closer to what you want that with a little help from the original (so it's not wasted after all!) you can *revise* the new one into final draft copy.

When you've actually reached the stage of final draft copy, you are ready to prepare your final draft manuscript. Whether you in fact submit it to a publisher for consideration, you should finish the job you started back in chapter 1 by seeing your story through to presentable final copy. Proper manuscript form isn't hard to learn. There are a few requirements, and a few elective options.

As for the musts, all fiction manuscripts should be typed on 8½ by 11-inch plain white paper, using black ribbon and a conventional type face. Do not use either heavy "erasable" bond or lightweight "onionskin." Margins should be about an inch and a half all round. Number pages consecutively in the upper right-hand corner, except for the first, which is unnumbered and carries your name and address, single spaced (the only single-spacing in the whole manuscript) in the upper left-hand corner, and your story's title, centered, a few lines lower down. The text of your story should begin approximately four lines below your title. Don't prepare a separate title page—it wastes paper and looks pretentious. And don't write "-30-" or "The End" or "Finis" at the end of your story. If you're actually worried that readers may not know when it's over, you can number your pages "2 of 12," "3 of 12," etc.

As for the optionals, you may wish to provide an estimate of the story's length, though editors tend to be rather suspicious of authorial counting. When it comes to the number of words they claim for a story, authors can be surprisingly modest. If you wish to include such an estimate, it normally goes in the upper right-hand corner of page one.

With typewriters becoming more and more sophisticated, the day is probably almost here when italics will be routinely typed *in italics*. But conventional practice is still to indicate them by underscoring. Space can't be italicized and thus, technically, ought not to be underscored, but I've never known an editor to reject work for so minor an imperfection in form.

Many typewriters/computers now also permit right-hand margin justification; some word processing programs even "choose" to justify the right margin; but you'll be better served by keeping your right margins ragged. Straightening both margins seems a little presumptuous, as if you're trying to point out how good your story would look in print. Most editors would be indifferent to such a "serving suggestion," but some few might resent it just enough to feel they need to look all the harder for imperfections in your "preset" story. Some computer justification puts spaces between words in a random and irregular way (unlike true proportional spacing which allocates space evenly across a line), so that in your effort to look "professional" you only end up looking peculiar.

As for corrections, minor typographical errors can be neatly done in ink. Punctuation marks can also be added easily, but if you need to take them out, use standard proofreading symbols (to be found in many handbooks and some dictionaries). Larger changes are best done on the typewriter and inserted as extra pages, letter coded sequentially according to the page they extend: 6, 6a, 6b, 7, etc. If you reduce the number of pages, renumber everything appropriately so that no one will think pages are missing.

One last recommendation: before entrusting your precious story to the mail service or otherwise letting it out of your hands, make copies of it. "Hard" copies, that is: on-paper copies. Computer disks have been known to crash. Anything magnetic can get demagnetized. Paper isn't indestructible either. But if you have several paper copies scattered in different locations, your chances of losing your work permanently and irretrievably are greatly lessened. It may seem unfair, after all the work you've put in, to have to spend time and money having your manuscript photocopied. But look on the positive side: photocopying is actually pretty cheap and readily available in most parts of the world. If you really can't afford it, or if it isn't available to you, good old reliable carbon paper still works. You can even make carbon copies on a computer's printer if you're willing to hand feed the manuscript page by page. However you do it, do copy your story!

Think of what you stand to lose: not just the hours of your life invested, but all the uniqueness of execution you could never recover, once lost. Think of poor Thomas Carlyle coming home to find that his housekeeper had pitched his manuscript of *The French Revolution* into the fire. A doughty Scot, Carlyle wasn't about to be beaten by a foolish servant and set about at once rewriting the whole book. On finishing this second writing he insisted the book had been improved by the accident. After what's been said about revision in this chapter, we can't very well argue with that. But who can say how much pure gold was lost as well? Your story might be the better for your tossing the version you've just finished and redoing the whole thing from scratch. But the effort would be inconvenient and painful. Then too, you might not have Carlyle's determination to carry on, and so your story might end up never being told. So don't ever give an "only copy" of your story to anybody, ever, for any reason—it's recklessly courting disaster.

• ten •

VARIATIONS ON THE THEME

NOW THAT YOU'RE A STORY WRITER . . .

You may remember being told, back in chapter 1, that after doing a story or two according to the *Primer*'s prescription, you'd be ready to craft further stories using a variety of different procedures. This chapter takes a look at some of those other "nine and sixty ways of constructing tribal lays." Of course it would need another whole book to inspect them in detail, but you're now a qualified fictional explorer secure enough in your skill to manage new trails on your own with a minimum of risk.

Two main things should be kept in mind when trying out any of the new approaches discussed here: (1) you've made this climb before, *but* (2) not from this side. That way you'll undertake the project with confidence, but not too much confidence. You'll find that just being a fiction writer with one or more completed stories under your belt really does help you feel assured. Knowing in advance how demanding it is to write a short story lets you gear up mentally for the job and pace yourself sensibly as you work your way through the many stages of the composition process.

But this very confidence can spell trouble for you. With so much of the process seeming so familiar, it's easy to forget that you haven't actually done a story this way before. So stay alert, proceed with caution, watch for curves, and be prepared to stop. Each of the many different starting points for stories has its special uses and strengths, but all of them have their risks too. This lesson will attempt to acquaint you with the most important of those strengths and risks.

STARTING FROM CHARACTER

The basic *Primer* story begins with a situation—a turning-point incident. But the main feature of that incident is a central character, whose values are challenged by, whose life is deflected by, a crisis. So, to use character as your starter ingredient ought to feel closer to the *Primer*'s opening strategy than most other approaches. For this reason it should prove a comfortable variation for your first venture into new territory.

The principal advantage of starting with character is that it is, after all, the basic ingredient in most fictional recipes. Whatever else fiction is, it is certainly people. Even if a story doesn't spend much of its time clarifying its characters' motives or values, it must make readers care about what happens to them or an account of their experiences simply isn't going to seem to matter. Well then, you may ask, if I have to get character right, why not always begin by figuring out my story's people and just let the story's meaning grow out of that understanding? Because different kinds of stories grow differently. All stories need interesting and functional characters in order to keep readers involved and the plot developing, but as this whole chapter is designed to show, good stories can grow from various kinds of seed.

Most long fiction does seem to originate in character. The longer the story, the more time the reader has to spend with a set of characters, the more essential that those characters' personalities have enough depth, integrity, and vigor to sustain interest. Because short story writers work in a tighter timeframe, they must pay at least as much heed to choosing just the right situation and showing just the right scenes as they do to delineating character. Thus, although character can be a good starting place for a short story, it's certainly not the only satisfactory one.

So then, how do you go about starting a story from character? You already have the tools at hand from chapter 3's discussion about how to turn an actual person into a fictional character. You may want to go back and take another look at those pages now. That "Checklist of Personal Characteristics" always helps firm up a character's personality profile. But the most important thing to remember is that a fictional being must come alive in your imagination. However you get them there, characters have to move into your head before they can get into your story.

Sometimes these imaginary people just seem to pop into your mind fully grown. More often they have to be assembled there, bit by bit. Often they grow out of real-life persons, as they must in your basic *Primer* story. Occasionally they are total fabrications, coming from who knows where for who knows why. But no matter where they come from or how easy or hard they may be to get settled in the world of your imagination, settled they must be by the time you introduce them into any story of yours.

Once a character actually exists in your mind, finding a story to tell about him/her should be easy enough—right? Well, that depends. Everybody's life is packed with story potential, including the lives of fictional beings. But just as we flesh-and-blood folk don't have a story-worthy experience every day, imaginary persons aren't automatically enthralling to watch and listen to either. Novice writers sometimes assume that all they need do is to deploy a fascinating creature and readers will follow it anywhere. Unfortunately, in fiction as in life, interesting is as interesting does. The fascination of your fascinating creature will wear off in a hurry if it does nothing but meander aimlessly around town day after day.

So you'll need to look through your character's life for a day or a week when something especially interesting happens, something significant occurs. Does this begin to sound familiar? It ought to, because from this point on, you're putting a story together the way *The Primer* had you do it. Use the same guidelines to locate a turning point and deflection, project a resolution, fill in the expository foreground, and you've got your story.

The only difference in starting with character rather than situation is that you let the personality of your imaginary being dictate the sort of circumstances your story will deal with rather than letting the nature of the crisis determine the sort of characters you will depict. Thus if your invented character is a middle-aged, overweight, timid, teetotaling male forest ranger, you've automatically eliminated all possible situations that lie outside his experience. This is not necessarily a disadvantage. But every starting point simply does eliminate all other starting points, which only means that, happily, there's an infinity of stories to be told.

THE RISKS OF STARTING WITH CHARACTER

First of all, you must make sure that the character you choose to start with is indeed a fictional entity and not a biographical sketch of some real-life relative or friend or enemy. If you don't escape from the actuality of flesh and blood right from the start, you may find yourself held captive by the literal "truth" of a real being. Your loyalty to the memory of this person will certainly narrow your imaginative scope and keep you from seeing possible "character improvements" which could increase the effectiveness of your plot or deepen the significance of your theme.

The main risk of writing character-driven stories has already been mentioned. If you let your character decide what he wants to do with your story, he may not feel like doing anything useful. You have to make him live through a part of his life that will have significance for your readers. Without significant action, you will have a character sketch but no story. If your character is interesting, it will probably be an interesting sketch, but it still won't be a story.

Another potential problem in character-generated fiction comes from the same source. If a writer concentrates on cultivating "character values," he may possibly neglect other values—plot, setting, theme, whatever. Even if he does manage to turn it all into a story, it may be an ill-proportioned story with too much analysis of motive and too few events, too many abstract interior commentaries and too few dramatic scenes with too little dialog. Such a story may feel "profound," but if readers find it tedious then all its profundity will count for nothing.

What it comes down to is this: Character is a very potent fictional element, one you need to take great care with when using it as kindling to get your creative fire going. Once lit, it has a way of burning faster and hotter than you're ready for and gutting your story before you even know what's happening. One of the anecdotes you often hear professional authors tell on themselves is how some character just "took over" a story they were working on and seemed to write it for them. What they don't often go on to mention is that such takeovers are usually disasters that have to be salvaged by painful rewriting that gradually cuts the pushy character back down to size.

This is not to discourage you from taking a character as your point of origin. Properly managed, character can be an excellent starting place. Many great stories have sprung from precisely this source. And of course, as already pointed out, you have to define character before your story can really begin to take shape, so that even if you don't begin with it you have to deal with character early on anyway. But you do need to use a lot of caution in handling character as a starter to make sure that you keep control of your story's development. Characters don't write stories, writers do. However smart some invented being may seem, he doesn't really know a thing about what makes a good story, so that if you let him do as he pleases he'll make a hash of things.

Which doesn't mean you don't "listen" to your characters and let yourself be "guided" by them. Once your characters are developed to the point of seeming to have an independent reality, they will certainly "tell" you what they can and cannot do, what they will and will not say. Like responsible actors in a play, they can help you as writer/director make your story come across to your audience in a convincing way. But you must never give in to the silly myth about characters actually seizing power and taking the fate of the story into their own hands.

STARTING FROM SETTING

If you are strongly affected by the "atmospherics" of physical environments, you will probably find that settings strike your imagination as theater stages just waiting to have dramas played out on them. An urban slum seems rife with potential violence. The dusty main street of a frontier town begs for a gunfight. A foggy night in London can still call up the Victorian world of Ebeneezer Scrooge or Sherlock Holmes. Backwoods hill country, tallgrass prairie, desert saltflats, bayou swamp—each has its special "regional" flavor that gives any story set there a quality uniquely its own.

Setting-generated stories tend to dramatize Humanity's struggle against the forces of Nature. At its best, as in London's "To Build a Fire" or Crane's "The Open Boat," environmental fiction uses Nature to reveal things about its characters that they could not reveal through ordinary interaction with one another. We feel that only in the chosen setting could the intended point of the story be adequately made.

Of course placing characters in clinically controlled settings is a favorite tactic of the fictional propagandist with a case to argue: for example Huxley's *Island* or Golding's *Lord of the Flies*. S-F (speculative fiction) writers make much use of setting—especially alien settings like *Dune*'s—to establish an otherworldly environment for their stories to unfold in. A Gothic thriller or ghost story frequently opens with atmospheric mood music ("It was a dark and stormy night"). And historical fiction tends to begin with word pictures of the bygone era to be presented.

All of which leads us to the biggest difference you'll find in starting from setting instead of situation or character: *setting always wants to come first*. Since its usual purpose is to provide a sense of place for action to happen in, setting usually gets its greatest emphasis in a story's opening paragraphs. Meaning that it's part of the exposition rather than the crisis phase, and as chapter 8 made clear you can do a better job of exposition after you've already written the crisis.

So you may need to do a little more skipping back and forth in time when working from setting. You'll probably find, once you have your world firmly established with a few paragraphs of "atmosphere" and your characters start arriving on the scene, that the crisis they're headed for begins to take shape clearly enough for you to jump ahead and write that scene. Once it's done you can probably write the resolution as well, before going back to finish up the exposition.

But sometimes a story's environment is too strong to be set aside this way to make room for character development. In Conrad's "Typhoon," for instance, we sense that the power of the storm is the power of the story, literally driving it before the wind. Conrad may have had little choice but to take it as it came. If you find yourself caught up in such weather, don't fight it, ride it. Make as much sense of it all as you can. Attend to people's values and motives as lulls in the storm permit. But let it happen as it wants to happen. You can always come back and remedy defects in the exposition later.

HAZARDS IN STARTING FROM SETTING

The number one risk in starting your story from setting comes from what we've just been discussing—getting swept away. Just as character can stifle action and turn a story into a sketch, so setting can stifle character and turn a story into an escapade. An escapade, however exciting, isn't a story. No amount of noise or speed can make up for a lack of sense.

But haven't you just been told to let yourself be swept away by any storm that's too strong to resist? Yes, *and* to try making sense of it whenever it gives you breathing space. But if the storm is truly overwhelming, you'll probably end up more battered than educated by it and with nothing especially wise or original to say about it. So the message is: Try to avoid heavy weather. That is, don't make the mistake of thinking that *intense or extreme* settings are more likely than ordinary ones to yield strong stories. If you want to try starting a story from setting, take a piece of familiar turf—a city street jammed with traffic or the less traveled rural road, a hardware store or library or supermarket, a mall or a mill—whatever will allow you to keep control of the story's development and insure that all its elements get proper attention.

Another potential danger in writing out of setting is that your story can turn into a travelog. Such accounts are among the most commonly rejected by fiction editors, who usually can't take the time to explain that documentary accuracy and mood painting are no substitute for in-depth characterization and significant action. The thrills of your first trip abroad may make an exciting slide-show presentation for close friends, but fiction is a different kind of guided tour.

Finally, setting means description, and descriptions have a way of luring the prosiest of writers into flowery effusions. Something about the natural beauty of a pine forest or the manmade grandeur of Chartres Cathedral makes us feel that ordinary words just aren't up to capturing it, and so we reach out for what we hope is poetry but is usually only purple prose. Far from being the moving tribute we intend, our bouquet of plastic blooms may even seem a mockery of serious homage. Better fall short of giving that glorious sunset its full due than to let your enthusiasm overflow in gushy excess. Most readers like understatement, which asks to be improved upon, but resent—and reject—overstatement, which has to be cut down to size. Keep Chekhov's famous dictum in mind: "a true description of Nature should be very brief and have the character of relevance. . . . [S]eize upon the little particulars, grouping them in such a way that, in reading when you shut your eyes, you get the picture. For instance, you will get the full effect of a moonlit night if you write that on the milldam, a little glowing star point flashed from the neck of a broken bottle, and the round black shadow of a dog or a wolf emerged and ran . . ."

STARTING FROM THEME

Many story writers find it hard to take theme as their departure point. Some even consider it a totally wrongheaded game plan, one that puts cart before horse. Theme, they argue, is what stories grow *toward*, not *out of*. To use a thematic starter, they contend, is to decide on your story's meaning before it even happens, and that's bound to dull your sense of discovery and so stunt your story's growth. So goes the argument, and it can sound perfectly reasonable until you remember that some of the finest stories ever written sprang from thematic origins.

Still, it's easy to see why theme might be a difficult place for some to begin. Themes are abstract and generalized, so they don't have the same specific substance as characters or settings. Love, death, duty, dignity—until we give them a particular time and place and body to inhabit, they don't have any concrete reality. So that if you like to stand firmly on solid ground and see the world of your story clearly around you from the beginning, the hazy uncertainties of theme are going to make you uneasy.

But it is this very shapelessness that appeals to some writers. Henry James almost always started with a thematic kernel (what he called his *donnee*, his "given") that he used as a basis for speculating about the details of his story. For him, the overall design of an artwork came first. The purpose of setting, character, and plot was to express that design. James found nothing limiting or inhibiting about working from an idea. On the contrary, by not starting out with a whole load of particulars, he felt freer to speculate about what particulars he needed to make his case.

FROM THE GENERAL TO THE SPECIFIC

In these days of scientific method, we all seem to get more practice at *inductive* than at *deductive* reasoning. We're expected to draw conclusions from statistics but not make up examples to support our points. But if you're going to theme-start a story, you'll need to exercise your deductive powers to the full. Obviously the first thing you need to begin a theme story is a theme. As long as it's a subject you're interested in, almost any subject will do: money, crime, freedom, politics.

Next, narrow your chosen theme (say, money) to a thesis: The love of money is the root of all evil; or, Money is the real proof of worth; or, Money tests the integrity of character. Note the difference between theme and thesis: theme is concept or principle; thesis is a statement of principle, a generalization about life. It must be a statement you yourself believe to be true. So that only if you truly do believe avarice to be the source of all evil should you try basing a story on that thesis.

Let's say you settle on "Money tests the integrity of character." That's still too abstract a thought to serve as the backbone of anything as solid as a story. So what you do is express it as a declaration with "people" in it: "People are ready to sell their souls if the price is right." Or, "People are grown up when they learn to manage money." This turns your abstract generalization into a concrete allegation. It's still not a story, but it's getting closer.

Next, cut that crowd of people down to just a single individual: Have John or Jane Somebody do something. "John sold his vote for a measly $2,000." "Jane put all her savings down on the new Jag before she started worrying about payments." Once you have your scenario this specific, you can begin filling it in with speculation: "John who? What vote? Why measly? Whose $2,000?" "Jane who? How much savings? Why *all* those savings? Why a Jag?" Etc. By the time you've answered the questions your single sentence prompts, you'll have a character (maybe more than one), a situation, a setting, maybe even a plot idea. And of course you'll have plenty more questions to follow up on—more leads than you'll need to build your story by *The Primer*'s familiar procedure.

STARTING FROM PLOT

It's hard to distinguish clearly between Plot and Situation as starting points. Plot may be defined as the story development plan that results from speculation about a hypothetical Situation. It is an abstract argument that requires characters in a setting (that is, a situation) to give it substance. For this reason it is hard to use, *independent of Situation*, as a generating principle, in *Primer*-style life-simulating fiction.

But suppose you have a gift, like Maupassant, for coming up with intriguing, unusual, and/or ironic sequences of events: A man adores everything about his wife except her liking for theater-going and cheap jewelry; when she dies, he finds out her jewelry is real, etc. If you get "plot" ideas like this, how do you deal with them?

If you're going to stick to *Primer* technique, and there's no reason not to, you'll do what Maupassant seems to have done—

flesh that abstract plot line out with some plausible characters who have understandable motives for what they do, and whose actions take on a meaning larger than themselves. The sooner you remove your plot idea from the realm of pure concept and give it recognizable human qualities, the better your chances of keeping the idea alive. Plots are mechanisms that work only if their machinery is compatible with the humans who have to operate them.

Starting a story from a plot idea has the same advantage noted earlier with regard to starting from theme: by being "outside" the physical constraints of character and setting, it allows for greater speculative freedom on the writer's part. But because it is even less tied to the rationale of human values than theme, it runs even greater risks of losing touch with human nature. Plot must be kept on a very short leash.

FLINT AND STEEL

That pretty well covers the alternatives to Situation as story starters: Character, Setting, Theme, and Plot—the four traditional "elements" of fiction. But there is one other alternative opening strategy worth mentioning. It doesn't really fit into any theoretical category, but it's a technique so commonly practiced by all breeds of fiction writers with such success that it shouldn't go unnoticed. Call it what you will, Flint on Steel or Creative Collision, the idea is simply to bring two unrelated bits of story matter together and see what happens. It's like playing with a chemistry set, pouring a test tube of substance X into a flask of substance Y. What happens may be nothing or may be an explosion. Most often it's something in between: the mixture fizzes, goes syrupy, turns green.

Whatever its exact nature, the substance is something new, a hybrid synthetic that can be as different from its parents as water is from hydrogen or oxygen. Whether it's a substance of actual worth will depend—as with any discovery—on its discoverer's being able to see the use of it. Don't expect this "blender" principle to work magic for you. The magic of fiction is something you have to engineer yourself. But this joining of diverse matter will sometimes enable you to see things you hadn't seen before, or at least see old things in new ways. That can make the difference between frustration and breakthrough.

There are no rules to tell you what can and can't be mixed. Since you'll probably be combining scraps and leftovers from your notebook that you haven't found any other use for, you've really got nothing to lose but a little time. If you're already stalled, which you probably are if you're resorting to making hash, you were already wasting time anyhow. This isn't to say that picking two ideas at random will work just as well as a more thoughtful selection, only that it's hard to predict what will work. So when you're stuck and you've tried every reasonable starting point, maybe it's time to be unreasonable.

I once linked a series of eerie experiences I'd had into a loose narrative that ended up as a published story. Another story came out of an unlikely crossbreeding of domestic melodrama and science fiction that offers a combination of futuristic innovation and plain old-fashioned human cussedness. The fact that it's still unpublished points up one of the potential weaknesses of this way of generating stories: your diverse elements may fail to overcome their differences and blend into a unified whole. I personally think my futurist family feud works, but so far haven't found an editor who agrees with me.

It's also not a good idea to include, on a regular basis, so large a measure of accident into what ought to be a deliberate and thoughtful process of craftsmanship. The famous canvas painted by a donkey's tail swishing at random is an amusing instance of art by accident, but it didn't start a donkey tail movement because it wasn't a responsible, or even a reliable, way to paint. So don't cook up fiction stew unless you don't have any—repeat, any—better ideas for making a story.

• eleven •

OTHER APPLICATIONS

A STORY IS A STORY IS A STORY

Chapter 10 looked at a number of different starting points for stories of the same basic kind *The Primer* helped you write in chapters 1-9—that is, stories of ordinary people living here and now. But "*Primer*-basic" isn't the only kind of fiction. This chapter will discuss some of the alternative story forms open to you, and how *The Primer* can help you write them.

But before turning away from *Primer*-style, normal everyday reality, a reminder: leaving the familiar world of your experience doesn't suddenly repeal all the rules of fiction *The Primer* has laid down. No matter where it happens (your own neighborhood, Timbuktu, the moon) or when (late twentieth century, early twelfth, or mid-thirtieth) a good story still has to have the same primary ingredients. If your characters aren't interesting and nothing much happens to them, you can't expect readers to care much for it.

Leaving *Primer* standard time and space is a little like taking a trip to a foreign land. There are important differences between life as lived in your hometown and as lived in that other country you intend to visit. You'll want to be able to follow the advice, "When in Rome, do as the Romans do." So you'll need to understand the special conventions of "Roman" culture before you set off. But for all their differences from you, other humans are going to be more like you than unlike you. Most worlds of alternative fictional reality are more like *Primer* reality than unlike it. So don't let leaving home go to your head. With a few exceptions, as noted below, your storytelling manners needn't change much from one country to another.

THAT BIG DIFFERENCE

It is generally agreed by writers, editors, critics, agents, and other fiction experts that the realm of the short story is a divided one, that some sort of fence stands between traditional/conventional fiction (the "serious" kind you study in school) on the one side and category/genre fiction (the entertaining kind you read for fun) on the other. But getting these same experts to agree on where that fence is and just what it's made of seems to be impossible. Part of the difficulty is that each "school" of writers is turf-proud enough to champion the rightness of its own practices with a biased, and hence distorting, zeal. Mainly, though, it's that each school so regularly poaches on the other's preserves, the fence seems to be down as often as up.

This doesn't mean that the fence either isn't really there or doesn't really count. The fact that each side is so vehement in pushing the legitimacy of its territorial claims shows how serious this border dispute is. The purpose of any definition should be to distinguish the differences between things more clearly. Of course no definition ever wins universal approval. Tens, even hundreds of exceptions to it are invariably cited. But a definition is of real value all the same if it helps those who apply it to draw useful distinctions.

It's not especially useful to put a fence between "slick" and "quality" fiction. Might as well divide stories into "good" and "bad," or "strong" and "weak." Such highly subjective distinctions are simply judgmental labels that define individual preferences rather than fictional qualities. After all, no writer strives for a "bad" or "weak" story. All seek "quality." The sort of definition we are looking for is one based on identifiable differences in purpose and/or approach.

Fortunately, just such a distinction has been common to literary criticism for hundreds of years. Back in 1595, Philip Sidney noted that the two principal ends of mimetic (life-imitating) art were "to delight and to teach." These are still its dual goals, and most stories of whatever kind try to do at least some of each. But the *emphasis* changes from one side of the fence to the other: on the category side it's mainly "delight"; on the conventional side, mainly "teach."

In other words: Category fiction seeks to divert with spectacle; conventional fiction seeks to educate with object lessons. Category fiction turns our attention outward toward the show on the stage; conventional fiction directs us inward toward reflection and/or self-analysis. Category asks us to slip into its alternative world for a brief vicarious experience; conventional fiction keeps reminding us of the real problems we have to cope with.

This explains why category fiction is sometimes loosely called "popular" or "mass market" or "broad appeal," whereas conventional fiction gets labeled "academic" or "literary" or "serious." Presumably not everyone feels the need for an ongoing education, but all of us, however solemn or work-oriented, do take in the occasional ball game or circus or parade.

WHY THE DIFFERENCE MATTERS

What this comes down to for a writer is that category fiction is harder to handle technically than the traditional sort, because it's tough to keep the reader's mind so occupied with spectacle, so engaged with entertainment, that it doesn't have the time to turn in on itself. Put another way, because of its specialized appeals category fiction runs greater risks than the usual garden-variety sort. If it fails to deliver the spectacle its specialist audience expects, it falls flat on its face. It is fiction without a net. A conventional story's appeal, being spread over the whole range of fictional elements—character, theme, plot, setting, style—has all different kinds of relevant data available to it. Its audience also expects it to be "educational," and education doesn't have to be as riveting as spectacle in order to be counted successful.

This is why you have spent ten chapters learning conventional fiction-writing technique before trying your hand at category. You needed a thorough grounding in the fundamentals of fiction rhetoric before attempting the stiffer challenges of the specialized genres. But though it is fiction without a net, though its specialist readers have highly selective needs that you must satisfy if you would succeed, there's no reason you shouldn't walk its high wire and earn the crowd's applause. You simply need to know what your audience wants of you so as to provide the right goods, and to be aware of the hazards so as to guard against them.

Just keep reminding yourself, category fiction readers are out for entertainment, and category fiction's job is to entertain them. Entertainment can come in many different forms—thrills, mystery, excitement, laughter. These are the "right goods" of category fiction's various genres. To call such goods "cheap" or "shallow" is as foolish and narrow as to defend them as the only worthwhile goals of any story. Affirming category fiction's purpose doesn't involve denying or disparaging that of conventional fiction, or vice versa.

Remember too that most fiction readers enjoy both conventional and category fiction, and look to each sort to deliver its own particular benefits: conventional fiction its object lessons; category fiction its action, pace, color, entertaining spectacle. This doesn't mean that a conventional story totally neglects the virtues of category fiction, or that category completely ignores the elements of conventional. As mentioned before, it's a matter of emphasis. You must give readers the emphasis they expect or you run the risk of forfeiting their interest.

Of course there are famous "Trojan horses" from both camps: Walter Van Tilburg Clark's *The Oxbow Incident* is a conventional novel dressed out as a category Western; John Updike's *Couples* may read like conventional fiction for a few pages because its style is fairly "literary," but it is actually more interested in the spectacle of its characters' marital infidelities than in understanding their motives or involving readers in their predicament. It's hard to say whether *The World According to Garp* is conventional fiction pretending to be sensational, or category fiction that occasionally flirts with being literary. What such interesting and exceptional cases prove is that rules can sometimes be broken successfully. But your chances of success are much better if you follow than if you break the rules.

You may recall from chapter 3 that fiction readers want to be led, want to believe what you tell them. This holds just as true for category fiction readers as for those of conventional stories. Category readers tend to be especially eager to see all the one-of-a-kind sights you can show them. In general, category fiction permits a much greater allowance of "extreme" material than conventional fiction can, in the interest of keeping the spectacle alive. So if your head is well stocked with the weird lore and legends of your special world, you will find your readers anxious to have you cast your magic spell of enchantment and hypnotize them into dreams.

Clearly, your first order of business must be to study and explore your alternative world to the point that you know it as well as your own backyard. What makes Frank Herbert's *Dune* or Larry Niven's *Ringworld* so credible is that their authors' conception of them is both complete and concrete. Louis L'Amour's sagas of the Old West seem real because in his mind L'Amour has gone back and *lived* there. P.D. James's Detective Inspector Adam Dalgleish does a convincing job of criminal investigation because James herself has done a thorough job of learning how Scotland Yard's C.I.D. works.

Some alternative environments are nearer normal than others, and so less difficult to research. We will consider the various types of category fiction roughly according to this scale of difficulty, from closest to mainstream to farthest away from it.

THE ACTION/ADVENTURE STORY

Depending on how amazing your adventure story is, it may be not so much category as conventional with breathtaking backdrops. One of the best stories ever published by *Kansas Quarterly* (a magazine I help edit), "It's Always Good in the Mountains" by Steven Allaback, is just such an adventure story. A gripping account of a climbing expedition, its mounting suspense results almost entirely from the steady buildup of tensions *within* the three members of the party and the corresponding increase in the chances of some accident occurring as a result. The story makes no deliberate effort to thrill or scare, but merely reports with relentless candor the mainly *internal* challenges the climbers must face at each stage of their venture. The mountain setting serves to raise the stakes by dramatizing the perils of having a battle of wills in such terrain, but the landscape never engulfs them. The personality clash remains the focus of attention.

If you want to write that sort of adventure story, you need only go back to chapter 10 and read about starting from setting and/or character. The pure category action tale's objective is something else: to keep a chain reaction of exciting events going like a tumbling row of dominoes, every fresh development triggering a further one until a full measure of forward thrust has been achieved. It's the equivalent, in a written-out story, of the adventure movie, "Raiders of the Lost Ark." The surest way to secure such momentum is, first, give your main character a quest that's fairly easy to explain but fairly hard to accomplish and second, invent a set of increasingly severe obstacles for him to overcome.

In adventure fiction, the hero's quest is all-important. It is usually the prime clue to his character: if noble (like Galahad's quest for the Holy Grail), we accept him as worthy of respect and pull for him; if wicked or paltry (like Gollum's quest for power in *The Lord of the Rings*), then we class him as a villain and root against him. Quest is motive: had Galahad sought the Grail to sell it to the highest bidder, he would be no hero; if Gollum had craved power only to share it with others, he couldn't serve as a villain in the piece. Quest is the action story's shorthand version of that bundle of traits you used to develop your character B in chapter 3. Villains very seldom make satisfactory heroes, so our discussion will confine itself to traditional heroic behavior.

Since adventure fiction has little or no time to pause for reflection, you must be able to work in motivation on the run. Action heroes more often show us in deeds than tell us in words what their priorities are. When they do speak, it's because they have something vital to say. And since they're always busy chasing or being chased, scuffling or dodging or just plotting their next move, their speeches are usually brief and basic. Their lack of time for talk and thought might seem to make it hard for you to reveal enough about them to keep readers interested, but actually it makes your job easier in a way because action heroes can speak and think in clear, bold words that let readers know exactly where they stand straight out.

As with your *Primer* story, an adventure tale usually grows best out of a situation. But unlike a *Primer* story, you'll want this situation to be loaded with the explosive intensity of a life-or-death struggle: danger, uncertainty, high stakes. The crisis will still be a "turning point" experience for the character, but rather than a change in his attitude it should bring a change in his fortunes. Imagine your hero at his farthest distance away from the successful completion of his mission, that dismal moment when all seems lost, when he can either capitulate or pick himself up and try to soldier on. Crudely put, it's when Popeye looks to be down for the count but with a last desperate effort he reaches out and grasps the can of spinach. This "Popeye turnaround," in one form or another, is crucial to the effect of most adventure fiction, which seeks to provide achievement thrills of the kind sports fans yearn for: the great comeback win against seemingly overwhelming odds. In fact, the "sport story" is usually just action/adventure in a sport setting.

Having identified the low point of your hero's fortunes, you can look forward to his final triumph and backward along the path of his descent in much the same way as you did in writing the conclusion and exposition for your *Primer* prototype story (chapters 6 and 8). But because this isn't "character" fiction, the obstacles your hero has to confront won't be his own conscience or errors of judgment so much as external causes, natural pitfalls, traps set by "the opposition." Yet even a pure action hero is more interesting and admirable if he shows some capacity to grow and improve, learning from adversity, adapting to changing circumstances, confronting his quest's problems and hazards with a steadily increasing effectiveness.

Ideally then, the action adventure story sets a strong and daring hero out on a risky and momentous quest. His goodness and resourcefulness may at first seem overwhelmed by the size of the task, and in fact at some point he will probably appear to have been defeated by the seemingly superior powers arrayed against him. But in an act of supreme determination he summons hitherto hidden reserves of strength (physical, mental, spiritual) and turns the tide of battle in his favor, routing the enemy (or whatever hostile forces may be) and marching on to victory.

THE WESTERN

Much of what has just been said about adventure fiction can be applied equally to category Westerns. Most Westerns are adventure stories in Western settings. A Western hero normally has the same sort of commanding physical presence and moral courage as an adventure hero, faces the same tough odds, and uses the same combination of shrewdness, daring, and sheer force to fight through to final victory. Western heroes are often badge-authority figures (sheriffs or marshals), though they may be more quiet leaders (scouts or guides), or even outsider/loners (solitary drifters or settlers) trying to build new lives for themselves by themselves. Whatever their actual calling, Western heroes know what they want and can usually find the way to get it—but without breaking their own stiff moral code or violating their strong sense of justice and fair play.

Westerns can be set in the present just like other adventure stories, but often they take place in the past century so as to exploit the vigor and color of the Old West's frontier days. When they do, they are actually a form of historical fiction, and must be researched as such. You must provide an elaborate descriptive context for this kind of story—the historical *what*, *where*, *when*, and *why* must be carefully and accurately defined (factual errors aren't readily forgiven by readers of historical fiction.) You'll find that doing all this will probably require more room than you have in a short story.

Which is why most Westerns run to novels, and why readers of Westerns have come to expect novel-length sagas. If you write "short" Westerns you should realize you'll be bucking the trend. Unlike most other genre categories, no ready market for Western short fiction exists, though Western stories do occasionally show up in regionalist publications and paperback anthologies. If you are determined to write Western short stories despite the doubtful market, stick to contemporary settings and issues that can be sketched in quickly, and leave most of your space for giving some color to your hero's personality and following his actions.

One hybrid version of Western can be fairly adequately managed in short story form—the wilderness survival tale. By using a familiar setting (Nature), a familiar antagonist (natural forces), and a generic hero, none of which need much description to be understood, you can give your attention to deploying an elaborate set of circumstantial obstacles that the character must overcome to make it through his ordeal. Such a story inevitably emphasizes the hero's ingenuity in coping with natural challenges.

THE CONFESSION

A category confession focuses the reader's attention upon the poignant adversity of another human being's troubled life. But as with adventure stories, confessions aren't automatically category fiction. Dostoevsky's *Notes from the Underground* is a sort of confession—a first-person report of a sad series of events in its narrator's life; yet it is considered a work of "literary" fiction. Charlotte Perkins Gilman's "The Yellow Wall-Paper" seems to meet the category confession's requirements even better: an emotionally unstable woman, kept in virtual isolation by her insensitive husband, sets down her progressively morbid thoughts in a journal. But it too is counted an early masterpiece of feminist literary fiction.

What keeps such "confessional" stories from being category fiction is that for all their poignancy they're not mainly out to touch the reader's sense of pathos. To be sure, their emotional charge is a necessary component of their meaning; suffering is painful, and a witness of pain must feel it to validate it. But the pathos is only a part—and not the largest part—of the intended effect of such stories. Conventional fiction's teaching function requires it to look into the causes of things, explore motives, interpret the significance of the events it depicts, which usually means directing the reader's attention away from the spectacle and pathos of suffering.

Category confessions, on the other hand, deliberately concentrate their coverage on the emotional effects. Rightly done, such fiction can have genuine therapeutic value. Sadness can be relieved, for a time, through experiencing another's sadness. But pathos as spectacle is a tricky concept. Wrongly handled it can easily become exploitive and manipulative, which is to say pornographic. To play upon readers' emotional susceptibilities, to misrepresent the nature of suffering with a view to making it "interesting," is a travesty and a perversion of fiction's legitimate purposes.

So if the notion of inventing emotionally painful experiences and "recalling" them vividly enough to evoke your readers' sympathy makes you feel uneasy, then confession writing probably isn't for you. Writing without conviction doesn't just nag your conscience. It saps your sincerity and so gives your work a dishonest smell that leaves readers holding their noses too. The important point is, you must be able to respect what you write. The fact that confessions present some unique risks simply means that they offer some unique challenges. There is no reason why a confession need be less honest than another sort of story, provided you undertake it with due regard for its particular hazards.

What especially concerns us here is how the *Primer*'s story-crafting method can be adapted to serve the purposes of the category confession. Since its basic theme is undeserved suffering, you will need to establish both a sympathetic central character and a situation which stacks the deck against that character. Whereas most action-story heroes, like their readers, are men, confessions are directed almost exclusively to women readers and thus feature women protagonist/narrators. This means that your central issue, the source of your complicating action, should be one that most women can respond to, especially those likeliest to be readers of confessions—the solitary, withdrawn, lonely, and bereaved.

The great danger in writing fiction for this audience has already been referred to above: that of exploiting their natural sympathies, feeding their grief, and confirming their fears that life is no more than a dismal series of setbacks. Given the emotional basis of confessions, they must stir their readers' feelings and thus affect their readers' state of mind. Considering that some confession readers' emotions may be seriously depressed, it is the duty of confession writers to provide an optimistic view of life's potential. However hard the knocks your character suffers she should never be deprived of her faith in the likelihood that things will improve for her. A confession should therefore always end upbeat, in a spirit of affirmation.

Wherever your ideas for confessions come from, they ought to be as timely and topical as stories reported in the news. Most of your audience read confessions out of a desire to feel that they are not alone in their sufferings, that others share the burden of the world's injustice with them. If the problems your character faces are familiar to your readers, they will find it easier to identify with them and participate in the experience being narrated. Most TV soap opera scripts are powered by domestic and professional strife, heightened simulations of the sort of personal and family troubles we all know at first hand. Successful confessions rely on the same fuel.

The *Primer*'s procedure works well in generating effective confessions. You may even be able to start from a life situation, an experience told to you first- or second-hand. As with writing a conventional *Primer* story, you assume the role of "the other" person involved, in this case the distressed woman. But instead of transposing into third person so as to diminish the intensity of the point of view, you keep the narration in first person in order to concentrate the emotional impact. In other respects build your story according to ordinary *Primer* specifications, keeping in mind the importance of embedding a ray of hope in your crisis scene that can be picked up in your conclusion.

THE ROMANCE

First, a word of caution—if you're going to write category romance, you should know that most romance publishers provide highly specific guidelines to be followed by anyone hoping to place work with them. Such guidelines are obviously the first ones to heed, whatever advice you may get from other sources (including this one). Another caution: if your interest is in "period" romance, you most likely won't be writing short fiction. In order to provide the historical context necessary to make such fiction come alive, you will need the larger canvas of the novel. Of course what *The Primer* has to say about fiction generally applies with equal force to both novel and short story, but the formal requirements of the novel's structure are different enough from the short story's that you shouldn't use specific *Primer* procedures to write novels.

Much of what has been said about category confessions applies equally to category romances. Both concern themselves with depicting emotional situations, both are customarily voiced in first person, and both tend to favor the female perspective (though some romances are now being written from a male viewpoint). But where confessions provide painful recollections of sad times endured, romances portray the hopes and throes of love, especially those of courtship. As in any fiction, the characters must be credible, and the heroine/narrator in particular should be "reader-friendly" as well. But all must stay uncomplicated enough not to impede the flow of the story's events. The twists and turns of plot will naturally reveal characters' attitudes and motives to a degree; but the individuality of their personalities cannot be permitted to distract readers from the situational intensity of their predicament.

For this reason, characters in romances serve best when they are recognizable, reliable types whom readers can size up without much reflection as worthy or unworthy, deserving of approval or of disapproval. If the characters of a category romance are allowed to appear as "gray" mixtures of strengths and weaknesses, readers will begin considering the merits of those characters rather than paying heed to the developments of the story. At no time should category romance readers be asked to wonder whether a narrator/heroine or her hero actually deserve the happiness they seek, whether that happiness is itself a proper goal for them, or whether they might actually be better off without each other. If your story prompts such questions, it is failing to deliver the "romance" which category readers read romance for and is feeding a conventional fiction reader's appetite instead.

SUSPENSE/HORROR/THRILLER

The specific mission of the category terror tale is to scare. Whatever else it accomplishes, if it fails to make your readers' flesh crawl, their pulses race, their neck hairs rise, it's not doing its job. A good horror story should be too frightening to read alone at night.

The reason you don't read a scary story alone at night is that "alone" and "night" are both elements that contribute to the atmosphere of fear. Others include spooky weather conditions like moaning wind, enveloping fog, streak lightning, and thunderclaps; "live" noises like creaking doors or stairsteps, murmurings, whistlings, whinings; eerie, possibly supernatural, visual effects—glowing, oozing, or moving of objects that normally don't move.

You needn't be bloodthirsty or ghoulish to write good horror fiction, but obviously you can't be squeamish either. You ought to relish laying on the fearsome and the gruesome with a fairly heavy hand, and you shouldn't see anything wrong with readers getting kicks out of being scared. Like confessions, horror stories invade readers' zone of emotional susceptibility and their writers must therefore use this privilege with tact and delicacy. *Caveat emptor* ("Let the buyer beware") may be an acceptable garage-sale creed, but it is a poor excuse for wantonly and viciously assaulting your readers' minds.

The purpose of atmosphere in a horror story is to put readers in an apprehensive mood. But apprehension is only an appetizer. If it's not followed by a main course, your feast of terror will be a failure. It is not enough to tickle and tease. You must deliver. What makes a sufficient main course? Theoretically, something big enough to pay off what the set-up seems to promise, a real threat to your main character's life and/or sanity. The threat can be other humans (the usual antagonists in regulation thrillers), terrestrial monsters or evil spirits (in supernatural horror tales), or extraterrestrial creatures or forces (in science fiction terror/fantasies).

Motives can be almost anything (pure blood lust, hatred of humanity, revenge for real or supposed wrongs, sexual deviancy or other depravity or mental disorder), so long as they drive the antagonist with convincing malevolence and can be made intelligible and meaningful to the reader in not too many words. Terribly complex motives, being hard to explain, should as a rule be avoided, though some psychological murkiness can lend an edge of uncertainty to a character's intentions.

The antagonist in a horror story should ideally be wicked to the core. If not, the reader will begin to have reservations about feeling he/she/it deserves no better fate than total and lasting annihilation. What makes horror horrible is the idea of good being beseiged and possibly overcome by evil. Meaning that the category horror story's premise must be basically the same as that of the morality fable, in which Evil engages Good in a life-or-death fight.

So as to keep the story's value system firm, the line between the two ought to be kept clear and emphatic. If a sweet, innocent young woman is attacked and pursued by a loathsome-looking ogre, the reader's moral sense must be totally engaged on the side of the girl. Any doubt cast upon the goodness of the girl or the evil of the ogre complicates the purity of vicarious terror, turns the reader's attention away from the spectacle and redirects it toward those more ambiguous questions of right and wrong that affect his personal moral philosophy. By addressing such concerns the story gives up its simplicity of focus and insistent momentum in favor of conventional fiction's diffused emphasis, and so fails to satisfy its readers' desires.

Given its uncompromising morality and its abnormal emotional heightening, its use of shock tactics and nasty surprises and uncanny quirks of fate, its heroes and heroines who seem helpless against the dark forces arrayed against them and can only hope for Providence or luck to rescue them, the horror story is about as far from *Primer*-standard reality as you can get. True, as fiction it must live within the laws of fiction: the opening must present a convincing setting and a plausible situation with issues that readers can buy into; characters' motives must be credible and rational enough to earn a sensible reader's acceptance; complications must develop to a crisis, which must in turn be resolved in an emotionally satisfying way. So that in a general sense *The Primer*'s guidelines remain in force.

Nevertheless, in order to accomplish its purpose, a successful category terror tale has to defy *Primer* recommendations more often than it follows them. Which recognition provides the key to using *The Primer* to write horror fiction. Almost invariably when *The Primer* counsels moderation, category terror opts for intensification. Your setting, as noted above, should reek and glow and murmur and drip with sinister suggestiveness. Rather than any normal everyday core situation to begin with, you'll need something exceedingly grisly and/or macabre.

Your crisis can also be a sort of turning-point experience, although the "deflection" in horror fiction usually comes nearer to the end than to the center of the story. As in an action/adventure, this turning point will mark a change in your character's fortune or circumstances, not his outlook or motives. Still, though your protagonist may be totally virtuous, your antagonist strictly evil, as suggested above, this doesn't mean your characters need be generic. Your hero's bundle of qualities can be all virtues and yet be unique, and the varieties of evil are equally diverse. Category characters often seem larger than life because they lack the conventional character's "realistic" balance of attributes, but they need not be "flat" on that account.

MYSTERY/DETECTIVE STORY

One of the commonplaces about mystery story writing is that you have to do your plotting in reverse, starting with the ending and working your way backward to the opening. As *The Primer* has already made clear, the beginning of *any* story is better written after you've already narrated the central crisis which the exposition is supposed to set up. So whatever kind of mystery you write, you'll find that your practice at thinking and writing "backward" will prove helpful in plotting the series of clues and discoveries that prepare the way for and justify your final solution.

Your practice with limited third-person point of view will likely also prove useful, since the detective story normally restricts its "interior" coverage to the thoughts of the sleuth character alone, excluding those of all possible suspects in the case. Of course first-person accounts, either by the detective or by an associate (e.g., Dr. Watson), are not uncommon. But because of its overall flexibility, limited third-person remains the most popular point of view for detective fiction.

One of the most persistent conventions of detective fiction is that of the "master sleuth." From the days of Poe's Dupin and Doyle's Sherlock Holmes down to the present, writers have chosen to give detectives some of the most striking personalities in all of fiction. More so than any other story genre, detective fiction makes use of the "continuing character"—a police inspector or private investigator of great personal charm and professional competence whose exploits readers are eager to follow in story after story. If you write detective fiction, you will have to decide whether or not to create a master sleuth.

If you find it premature to be thinking in terms of a "continuing character" before you even write your first detective story, consider that what you're really thinking about is the kind of detective story you want to write. If what intrigues you about a mystery is the puzzle element—how applied intellect and/or diligence can solve a sticky problem—you could find attending to the ongoing demands of a developing fictional character burdensome. If on the other hand you are at least as interested in the way an investigator's personality affects his performance as in the case itself, you might prefer to study the progressive phases of an individual detective's career over a whole series of cases.

One final note: unless you're a detective yourself (or have been one), you'll have to learn how real investigators work, down to their professional habits and slang. Your particular detective won't conform fully to type, of course; but unless he seems real to your readers (many of whom will have insider expertise), he won't solve any cases, because they won't follow him beyond the first page. In a detective story, you absolutely must get "the facts" straight, since its validity depends on its squaring fully with well-established professional practices. Your detective may bend or break procedural rules on occasion, but you and he must know what those rules are, and let your readers know you do. Ignorance of the law is no excuse.

THE HUMOROUS STORY

Anecdotes, comic yarns, tall tales: America's storytelling history probably contains more fiction out strictly for laughs than any other country's. We're a nation known for joking, poking fun, exaggeration. Not surprisingly, many of our most popular TV series have been situation comedies—from "I Love Lucy" and "The Beverly Hillbillies" to "Newhart" and "Golden Girls." Television has stolen much of the popular humor market away from magazine fiction, but the funny story will always be an American habit.

The difference between category humor and the literary humor of Mark Twain or James Thurber is that whereas Twain and Thurber are mainly concerned with getting a satiric message across, one which humor helps them convey, the category humorist's goal is simply to keep readers amused. The success of humorous category fiction is measured by the same yardstick as that used for TV sitcoms or stand-up gagsters: if we laugh, it lives; if not, it dies. This makes category humor terribly hard to write—one flat paragraph can kill the hilarity and so ruin the whole effect.

Given such a risk of failure, you may wonder why anyone ever tries it or how anyone ever succeeds. Yet humorous narratives do keep getting written. Are there any tried-and-true devices that humor writers consistently count on? In particular, does *The Primer* provide any useful concepts that humorists can apply? This is not the place for a lengthy analysis of what makes people laugh. But we can take the time for a brief discussion of the main source of fictional humor and how to cultivate it.

That source is, in a word, incongruity. Nearly all visual humor comes from things looking odd, peculiar, "wrong": a very large woman embracing a very small man; a gowned and jeweled socialite taking a cream pie in the face; a pompous professor rocketing down a slippery slide. A pratfall is funny because someone's feet stop functioning normally and start to behave in a peculiar way, flying abruptly into the air, pulling the person's legs out from under him, sending him with a bump to the floor. Funny faces and figures, postures and gaits are funny mainly because of incongruity—huge ears on a tiny head; thin legs below a fat body. And of course much situational humor arises from sequential incongruity: things happen that seem outrageous, hence funny, in their violations of probability—so-called non sequitur ("it does not follow") humor.

Since *The Primer*'s approach to story construction emphasizes reasonable motivation and a logical development of action, it may seem a poor guide to the zany twists and turns of incongruity. But consider that things strike us as incongruous because they deviate from what we expect them to be like and we recognize such deviations as ludicrous. This means that beneath every incredibly ridiculous story lies a perfectly credible set of circumstances, cast of characters, series of events—an ordinary reality that tells us the absurd story is absurd. So if you're trying for incongruity, the best place to begin is with a *Primer*-style tale of ordinary reality. Once you describe the norm, you'll have established the "center" from which eccentric developments deviate.

FANTASY AND SCIENCE FICTION

Of all the places you can set a story, the worlds of fantasy and science fiction are surely the farthest from normal reality. It might seem that such environments, being so remote from ordinary reality, would follow their own exotic rules and live by their own peculiar laws, free from *The Primer*'s sort of mundane lore. But in fact no matter how distant the galaxy, how strange the culture, how alien the beings you choose to write *about*, that audience of earthlings you're writing *for* still has to be able to understand and care about your story in human terms.

Meaning that weirdness alone won't make fantasy or science fiction stories work. Of course weirdness is useful, even necessary to all forms of s-f (that is, "speculative" fiction, ranging from the carefully extrapolated hypotheses of "hard" science fiction on one end of the spectrum to the surreal conceptions of pure fantasy on the other). In order for readers to feel transported in time and/or space you'll have to give them a healthy dose of extraordinariness. S-f writers are fiction's seers and prophets, conjuring up visions of what may be or might have been, its oracles, wizards, witches. You must have a bit of magic about you to bring it off. And energy. Your enthusiasm for the wonders you report will help catch and hold your readers' attention. But it's not enough just to point and shout. You've got to be knowledgeable about this other land of your invention: all its weirdness has to be "brought home" to an audience that depends on you to serve as their guide and interpreter, to make its otherworldly events and entities comprehensible. Without a human frame of reference to give them relevance, alien life forms in an alien environment are subjects for scientific study rather than fiction readers' curiosity.

The Primer can help you provide just such a frame of reference. If your story uses a recognizably human being as its point-of-view character (as most s-f stories do), then working up that character's personality profile, in the same way you did for narrator B back in chapter 5, will be helpful. The character's personality will clarify the story's controlling attitude and therefore your readers' sense of the alien places your story plans to explore. If your story is told from a nonhuman viewpoint—unusual and very tricky—you'll have to find a graceful way to translate its alien perceptions into words your readers will understand. You must provide a human frame of reference without benefit of a human point of view (a step beyond Faulkner's task of using an idiot to tell part of *The Sound and the Fury* [see chapter 4, "Working in a Straitjacket"], hence technically very difficult).

Theme/thesis is normally of great importance in s-f. Some of its alternative realities seem to have no purpose other than to provide psychedelic mind trips or kaleidoscopic combinations of mood and color. But most s-f writers are drawn to the form mainly because it offers them a virtual blank slate to draw their dream—or nightmare—societies on, and therefore the greatest possible freedom to speculate about mankind's place in the universe. Like any other freedom, though, s-f's "blank slate" carries with it the added responsibility of using it to some purpose. The s-f reader assumes that the s-f writer invents an alien world in order to explore some aspect of life more effectively than he could using conventional reality. This means that thinking about your central character also involves thinking about what sort of "case" you want that character to make and how it will affect the story's overall theme.

The basic choice in telling a s-f story is whether to have it happen in a world very like, or very unlike, the one we know on planet Earth. That world may be Earth itself in some far-off future or some remote past, or even the present (an invasion from outer space, for example, normally occurs in "present time"). Or it may be on Alpha Centauri, or some universe beyond our own, or an alternative dimension or "time warp" reality. But wherever your story happens, you still have the same question to deal with: Is the socio-econo-political scene to be depicted going to resemble what we have here or differ strongly from it?

The answer to this question cues the next one: What sort of statement about the quality of life on present-day Earth does the depicted world make? That is, when you set contemporary Earth society side by side with your alien world's, what does it mean? As noted above, not all s-f aspires to serious social criticism, but because of the scope of its departure from normal reality and that resulting blank-slate status, it needs "message" more than any other genre of category fiction in order to give it substance.

The basic *Primer* story explores a behavioral question by means of a central character's rite of passage through a life crisis. The basic s-f story inspects an Earth-relevant issue through a series of events that may not occur on Earth or involve Earthlings or even depict "human nature," but which end up all the same making a case, contributing in some fashion to one of mankind's ongoing debates about human values and choices. The blank slate invites allegory; in order not to seem empty and/or gratuitously exotic, s-f has to take seriously the object lessons it deploys. Thus, ironically, the genre of category fiction most remote from ordinary reality in its settings is probably the closest to conventional fiction in its goals and methods.

APPENDIX

SUPPLEMENTARY STUDENT STORY

1. Narrative A (Chapter 2)

When the tin bell tinkled, I looked up and watched the young man come into the deli. He just stood there by the door, hands in pockets, glancing nervously all around the shop. He was dressed in jeans and a plaid shirt with tails hanging out over his back pockets. I thought he looked like a divinity student.

Without seeming to glance at me he nodded as if in satisfaction and began drifting slowly toward where I sat behind the scarred and pitted wooden counter. But then he walked on past me with only a sidelong look at the old-fashioned ticket spindle, so I asked him if I could help him.

He seemed to scoff at the idea, then turned to face me at last. "Money," he said. "All of it. Now." Only then did he pull the small black handgun from its hiding place and start waving it in my face. He seemed as surprised as I was by what he was doing. Even with his gun he didn't really scare me, but I couldn't move.

He stepped quickly behind the counter and placed the gun

to my ear. It was extremely cold. Again he asked for money, again I stayed frozen in place. He wouldn't really hurt me, I thought, looking out the door at a beautiful sunset. "Don't move," he told me.

The register opened with a loud "ching-buzz" that made me jump. I started to turn to tell him that what he was doing was wrong, but he only reminded me not to move and started grabbing bills and cramming them into a brown sack. This is his first robbery, I thought, his first crime.

"I'm sorry," he muttered. "You seem like a nice lady. You just happened to be here." He wiped his hand on his jeans. "Now in there—move," he said, motioning to the open door of the john. He shoved me along, half-heartedly, pulled the door shut behind me, and told me to stay put.

Ten minutes later I came out into the empty shop.

2. Narrative B (Chapter 3)

I jerked open the deli's front door, letting in a long slash of sun across the floor and up the counter. Inside it was too dim to see anything except a spindle that seemed to glow white hot on the counter top. I stepped into the shop and waited for my eyes to adjust.

As soon as I could see, I headed toward the cash register. That was when I spotted the old lady behind the counter. Sure, it had to be somebody clerking the place, but why in hell a feeble old lady? Why did my luck have to run so bad? I told myself: just a mop upside down in a blue bag, no real person in there.

Walk along the counter, past the cash register, past that shiny spindle. *Could she help me*? She didn't know how funny she was. Then I knew if I was really going to do it, it had to be right away. So I spun round and said, before I could change my mind, "The money. All of it. Now." It sounded so stupid I almost laughed. And I hadn't even drawn my "gat."

I pulled out the cap pistol and pointed it at her, waving it back and forth to keep her from seeing it was a fake. She just stood there, so I stepped behind the counter and jammed the pistol to her ear and told her again to get the money for me.

But she didn't move. I'd have to open the register myself.

She started turning to face me, and I didn't want that, so I told her to stay put. Just a dust mop upside down in a blue dress, I reminded myself. Hit the buttons—ching-buzz, bingo! Must be a hundred bucks there. I crammed money into a brown sack, thinking I must look pretty stupid.

I pointed at the john and told her to get inside it. I was pulling the door shut when my shirttail seemed to catch on an invisible nail, and for a second I stuck there. "You seem like a nice lady," I said. "You just happened to be here, that's all." Then I broke free.

3. Narrative C (Chapter 5)

Out of the silence, the tinkling sound of the tin bell rebounded off the neatly stacked cans. Sunlight slashed across the plank floor, up the counter front and across its scarred and pitted top, flaming the skewer of an old-fashioned ticket spindle.

The young man's shadow fell across the stripe of sunlight as he entered. Until his eyes adjusted, he could see nothing in the room but the abnormal gleam of the spindle. He closed the door behind him, making the bell ring again. Nervous, he stuffed his hands into his pockets, then jerked one back out to rub the furry stubble on his chin.

His narrowed eyes, rapid and alive, darted round the shop's interior, anxious to see. Was that another door in the back wall? Just an open john, smelling of cheap disinfectant. He nodded in satisfaction. That would come in handy later.

The dim interior came into view, a Polaroid picture. He swaggered up along the counter, past the cash register. The old woman clerk rose up ghostlike out of a chair behind the counter. Clara, from her name tag. Well, old Clara in a blue flower dress, too bad it has to be your shift. Someone's got to mind the store, but why not somebody else, somebody not so . . . what the hell, what do I care? She's nothing. Nothing but a rag mop in a blue sack.

The rag mop had a voice: "Can I help you, young man?"

He almost laughed. She didn't know it yet, but she was going to help him plenty. But where does she get off with this "young man" crap? Old bag.

His finger touched the spindle. He had to pick it up, feel the thin coldness on his hand. But stick to business. Tell her. Do it, now, you hear me?

He whirled around to face her. "The money. All of it. Now!" he shouted, feeling like an actor playing a tough guy in a bad movie. It didn't sound like he meant it, no real edge to his voice, just a dumb loud noise. She stared at him like she hadn't heard. Then he remembered he hadn't drawn his "gat." No wonder she was staring. No gun, no stickup. He pulled out the cap pistol and pointed it at her, waving it back and forth to keep her from seeing it wasn't real.

Still she stood there motionless. Had he scared her so bad? How could she be scared when it all was so ridiculous to him? But he couldn't waste time. Somebody could come in any minute. He ran round the counter, got behind her, touched the gun to her ear. "I said now," he muttered, trying to sound mean. Through the gun he could feel her body stiffen.

She started swiveling to face him, and he didn't want that. He wouldn't meet those accusing green eyes, mama eyes, again. "You stay put!" he commanded. But if she stayed put he'd have to get the money himself. It wasn't working out the way he'd pictured it back in his room.

"Are you sure you want to do this?" she asked him softly.

"Goddam, lady, you just shut up, hear me? I don't want to hurt you." He pushed her against the counter, transferred the gun from his right hand to his left, and stepped toward the cash register. Jesus, what's a dump like this doing with a computer? What key, Total? Subtotal?

The register tray shot open with a loud ching-buzz, the old woman jumped, and he felt like he'd won some kind of game. The payoff lay there ready for him to take, so easy. Ones, fives, tens. No twenties. Never mind, he didn't need a fortune. Just enough to take him away.

He saw a stack of brown sacks under the counter and they became part of his luck, part of the plan. He popped one open and set it on the counter beside the register. The bills felt dusty dirty to his clutching hand as he moved them from till to sack, so he rubbed the palm against his pant leg. His face began to itch, but he didn't want his fingers to touch it. Losing your cool, guy?

Too late to pull out now, get on with it.

"OK, now in there." He motioned at the open john, nudging her that way. He had to keep prodding her forward all the way to the wall beside the toilet. "Now just stand there quiet. If you start yelling, I'll come back and shut you up."

Slowly he backed from the foul-smelling room. A pressure on his hip, his shirt tail caught on an invisible nail, he hung there a long second, unable to move. A tug, a rip, he tore free. The woman began to turn toward him, to speak, to accuse.

He slammed the door shut. "You stay facing that wall," he screamed, trembling. He turned to leave, froze in his tracks, turned again to the door. "I'm sorry," he said, barely above a whisper. "You seem like a nice lady. You just happened to be here."

He thought he heard weeping on the other side of the door. He turned and fled.

4. Narrative D (Chapter 7)

Before stepping outside he decided he'd better stop and collect his thoughts. But his thoughts swirled and would not gather. He wiped sweat from his forehead with his shirt sleeve, noticed the cap pistol still in his hand, and dropped it into the money sack. Hugging the sack to his chest, he pushed the door open with his foot and went out.

It seemed colder than when he'd gone in, and the wind had picked up. He told himself not to run or act guilty or look behind him, but he couldn't help how he felt—alone, and sick. How much time did he have now? How long before the old bag called the cops?

He said he'd shut her up. Maybe he should have put her out. But he couldn't have hit her. He couldn't really hurt anybody, especially not an old woman like that, with mama eyes.

His boot turned, twisting his ankle, and he pitched forward falling on top of the sack, which he kept tightly clutched to his chest. For a few seconds he lay half sprawled on the cold cement. He panted to get his breath back, felt his gut churn and a bitter taste rise in his throat. Better find some place fast, he thought, staggering to his feet. He didn't get far.

Pain carved him with a glass cutter's edge as he grabbed for the corner of the gray stone building. He doubled over, retching violently. Yet in spite of the ripping and tearing in his stomach and his burning throat, nothing had ever felt so good. He spewed his system clean. Over . . . he thought, finally over . . . Standing again, he looked up to a weathered painted sign above his head: CAROL COU TY B S DEPOT.

His sack now pressed more to his stomach than his chest, he staggered inside and headed for the men's toilet. Somebody had scrawled a "Help Wanted" sign above the grimy urinals. With a wry smile he went into a stall and sat down on the stool. He let out a sigh of thanks for the privacy of toilet stalls and began to go through the contents of his puke-flecked sack.

Cap gun. Cap'n Cap-gun, that's me. Big shot, pow pow. He pointed the barrel at the ceiling and pulled the trigger, click click click. Oh, he was one dangerous dude, he was. Scaring old ladies. Being so scared by an old lady's eyes he had to throw up on main street. What kind of pantywaist pulled that kind of stunt? He wiped the toy with his shirt tail. Could it really matter if a cap gun had his fingerprints on it? Could fingerprints even stick to a cap gun? Everything seemed so stupid.

He lifted the lid of the toilet's water tank and dropped the gun into the scummy green water. Somebody'd find it in ten years, next regular cleaning. "Bye bye, Cap'n," he cooed at it, replacing the lid.

Now, how much bread? Lots of ones, not many fives or tens. A lousy seventy-eight bucks! Didn't come close to paying for all the sweat. He was tempted to flush the lot down the pipe and just walk away from this stinking town. If *he* didn't have anything on him, then *they* didn't have anything either. Except the old woman could finger him. She'd looked him over good. Damn! Why hadn't he covered his face? Because he'd been too dumb. He slammed his fist into the metal door of the stall and felt it shake on weak hinges. Everything in this town is falling apart, me along with it.

A fresh surge of nausea hit his stomach and he felt his bowels start to squeeze. He flung up the toilet seat and jerked at his belt buckle. *Can't afford to dirty my pants. No change of clothes here*. It felt like his body wanted to get rid of everything he'd dumped in it the past two days, flush out all the muck, start over clean. Gradually he relaxed, his shoulders hunching forward, his forehead against his palms.

Ten minutes later he reached out for the roller, found it empty and broken. A job for somebody . . . But what the hell was he supposed to do? The brown sack with the money in it lay at his feet. Just tear away the top of it. What a lousy waste of a lousy day.

He stood up, pressed the flush handle. Water roared into the toilet bowl and kept running. He jiggled the handle, but the water wouldn't stop. What difference did it make? It could run forever and not get anywhere. *Sounds familiar. So who cares? Let it go.* Then he remembered the gun. That's what was keeping the water running. He'd have to fish it out. Why? What difference did it make? He wouldn't be around. He was leaving. They wouldn't find it till he was long gone. So what did he care? He was clearing out. Yeah.

A bold splash of color, a collage of graffiti above the tank, caught his eye. "Call Mary for a good . . ." "If you're so smart, whatcha doing here?" "How many bankers does it take to screw a farmer?" One in particular stood out from the rest. Some would-be caricature artist had drawn President Reagan in a monk's cowl, wildly waving a sign that read: JUNKIE GO HOME! First he spat at it. Then he flipped it off. Then he laughed. Sure, why not? Takes all kinds of junkies to make a great country like ours. Hey, maybe I will . . .

Tucking his money into his shirt, he walked out of the stall and headed for the ticket counter.

5. Narrative E (Chapter 8)

The young man stared around his small apartment at the used furniture, the used TV, the empty tray with the remnants of last night's meal. "It's just the last straw," he said out loud to no one. His eyes shifted from the room's disarray to the faded photograph on the table beside him.

A grizzled old face in sepia tones stared back at him with a look of pride. "Donald," it seemed to say, "you did so good after your momma died . . . going off to that business college and all

. . . and you just a youngun yourself . . . I been so proud of you, boy!"

Yeah, Shakey, we had some high old times together, you and me. Sure do miss you, old man. Donald sighed, picked up the picture, and looked into those wise old eyes. *I always figured to come home in style. Buy a car and we'd go on the road again, a while . . . Maybe even go sit around a fire out somewhere and tell Captain Midnight stories, the way we used to.*

Donald remembered tales of a swashbuckling hero who robbed from the rich and kept the money. It never failed to make Donald laugh when he thought of the devilish gleam in Shakey's old eyes as he told of riches, women, and fun.

Gently, Donald set the photograph back on the table. *Now I don't know where I'm going. Can't go home with nothing to show for being away. Can't stay away with nothing to do to keep alive. Maybe if you'd finished that last story . . . Remember, there was a gun, and this woman, and of course Captain Midnight.*

How he'd begged Shakey to tell him what happened, and Shakey never would. "You're better off not knowing, boy." *I always tried finishing that one in my head, but I couldn't ever make it end right. Nobody could ever tell them like you, Shakey.*

Now he sat here on the edge of a squeaky half bed, lacing on work boots when he had no work to do. Got to get down to the *un*employment office for my weekly rejections, he thought, let them dump on me again. "And where do I find me some hope?" he said, kicking his old cardboard box of possessions so hard it tipped and spilled, scattering books and papers, unanswered letters and unpaid duns, over the floor.

Amid the clutter lay the gun he'd used to act out Shakey's Captain Midnight stories. " 'Tain't real," Shakey'd said, "but you ain't really Cap'n Midnight either." Remembering the old toothy laugh, Donald picked it up. For a cap gun it had a pretty real look to it. He slipped it under his shirt inside the waist of his Levis next to his skin. It felt cold as a real gun. In a rush he was out the door, down the stairs two at a time, off into the chilly March morning.

"Donald Kell, to see Miss Wilks," he told the bored receptionist behind the desk of the small receiving room of the employment office.

"Donald Kell to see you, Miss Wilks," she murmured in a faked sexy voice (who's she think she's turning on? Donald wondered) to the intercom. She pointedly avoided his eyes.

Instead of asking him to come in to her private quarters, she came out to him. *Afraid I'll dirty the furniture? Maybe she thinks I'd try to rape her.* She wore a frilly dress and had her hair done up fancy and she fidgeted when she talked. Donald almost laughed to think what Shakey'd have said. "Fussy old broad, ain't it, boy?" or maybe, "Suppose her face freezes up like that every winter?"

He bit his lip to keep his own face straight as she recited the litany of no's. "We have no jobs suited to your skills . . . No openings are anticipated in the near term . . ." No, no, no . . . we can't help you, we don't want you, go away, get lost—like he had leprosy, untouchable. He only half heard her as he turned and strode out the door. He tried to slam it but it shut at its own speed with a pneumatic hiss.

He stood on the curb staring along the empty gutter. What did you do when they wanted to waste you, send you to the sewer? Crawl away and find some dark corner to die in? Sit on the sidewalk and beg? He was getting thrown out of society by society. Like the guy in the book that nobody'd give a job, who ended up stealing a loaf of bread. Take your rights away and they take your conscience too. He walked off down the sidewalk.

The gun began to feel uncomfortably hard against his skin. And conspicuous. He bent forward, hunching his tall frame and sucking in his stomach to hide the bulge. Fragments of thoughts—huge stacks of money, bills stamped PAID in bold black letters—whirled through his mind. His boots thumped the cement dully. No trash on this sidewalk, nothing in this gutter, not even a wino. Talk about a tough town, not even winos can live here. *Wine be damned, what am I going to do for food?*

The dark gray shape of a small deli appeared to his right. An ideal place, if he really wanted to try out his Captain Midnight routine. No cars in the little parking lot, no one going in or coming out. Yeah, a good place all right. Beginners should start small. Still he waited.

A mangy old tom cat sniffed hungrily around the crack at the bottom of the deli's door. His coat was caked and matted and his yellow chest fur clung to his ribs. "Good hunting, old fellow,"

Donald called softly after him as the tom twitched his tail in seeming disgust and stalked off.

If it was ever going to be time, the time had come. *Take a deep breath,* he told himself, *and keep a stiff upper lip*. He closed his eyes and tried to summon up the old pictures of gold bullion and precious gems overflowing treasure chests. The picture would not form. Eyes still closed, he reached unwillingly for the door handle.

6. Finished Manuscript (Chapter 9)

Angela Wooley
P. O. Box ***
City, State ZIP

A Matter of Conscience

The young man stared around his small apartment at the used furniture, the used TV, the empty tray with the remnants of last night's meal. "It's just the last straw," he said aloud to no one. His eyes shifted from the room's disarray to the faded photograph on the table beside him.

A grizzled old face in sepia tones stared back at him with a look of pride. "Donald," he could almost hear it say, "you did so good after your momma died . . . going off to that business college and all . . . and you just a youngun yourself . . . I been so proud of you, boy!"

Yeah, Shakey, we had some high old times together, you and me. Sure do miss you, old man. Donald sighed, picked up the picture, and looked into those wise old eyes. *Always figured I'd come home in style. Buy me a car and the two of us'd hit the road again, a while . . . maybe even make us a fire to sit by, and then tell Captain Midnight stories, just like before*.

Donald remembered tales of that legendary swashbuckling hero who robbed from the rich and kept the money. It never failed to make him laugh, that devilish gleam in Shakey's old eyes as he told of riches, women, and fun. But more than anything else it was the excitement of doing something big and doing it right.

Gently, Donald replaced the picture on the table. It seemed like nothing was either big or right anymore. *I got no plans, you know? Can't go home—got nothing to show for being away. Can't stay away—got nothing to keep me alive. God, Shakey, where's that leave me? Maybe if you'd finished that last story . . . Remember, there was this woman, and this gun, and of course Captain Midnight.*

He'd begged the old man to tell him what happened, but he never would. It wasn't like Shakey's usual cussedness, either. He'd say, "You better off not knowing how that one goes, boy," nodding his head and sucking his teeth. Donald had tried finishing it himself, but never could make it come out right somehow. Nobody ever got them right like Shakey.

Now here he sat on the edge of a squeaky half bed, lacing up a pair of work boots knowing there was no work waiting for him to do. His only job was walking to the *UN*employment office for his weekly rejections, to get dumped on again. "And where do I find me some hope?" he asked the empty room, kicking his cardboard box of goods so hard it tipped over and spilled like a trashcan, scattering books and papers, unanswered letters and unpaid bills over the floor.

In the clutter lay the gun he'd used to act out Shakey's Captain Midnight adventures. " 'Taint real," Shakey'd said. "But then you ain't really Cap'n Midnight, either." He could still feel the horny old hand tousle his hair, the low, throaty chuckle that made everything seem fine. Donald picked up the cap gun. For a toy, it looked pretty real. He slipped it under his shirt inside the waist of his jeans. The metal felt cold as real gun metal against his skin. In a rush he was out the door, down the stairs two at a time, and off into his new day. The bright morning sunshine filtered through some hazy clouds, but the March wind was bitter and Donald swung his arms vigorously at his sides as he set a brisk pace toward the employment office.

"Donald Kell, to see Miss Wilks," he told the bored receptionist behind the desk in the employment office's small reception area.

"Donald Kell to see you, Miss Wilks," the receptionist murmured in a fake-sexy voice (who does she think she's kidding? Donald wondered) into the intercom. She pointedly avoided his eyes.

Instead of inviting him into her private lair, she came out to him. *Afraid I'll dirty her posh furniture? Or maybe try putting some moves on her? That'll be the day*. Miss Wilks had on a frilly dress and her hair was done up in a fancy swirl, and she fidgeted when she talked. She talked fast and jerky, and Donald almost laughed to think what Shakey'd have made of her. "Fussy old broad, ain't it, boy? You s'pose her face freezes up that way come winter?"

He bit his lip to keep his own face straight as she rattled off the string of no's. "No jobs suited to your skills . . . No openings anticipated in the near term . . ." No, no, no . . . Can't help you, don't want you, go away, get lost. Like a friggin leper, untouchable. Before she stirred him up bad, he turned and strode out the door. He tried slamming it behind him, but it shut at its own speed with a pneumatic hiss.

Standing out on the sidewalk, he stared at the empty gutter. When they won't even let you interview to pump gas, they're telling you to drop dead. Two years of college, what's that worth? Just enough to spit at. They were daring him to try something, like the guy in the book who couldn't get work and ended up stealing a loaf of bread. When you got nothing, you got nothing to lose.

Yeah, Shakey, you and me used to talk about pulling off the big job, but that was just woofing. Good story, but like you said, no way to live. You wouldn't want me to do it, would you, old man? Maybe if you were standing here as shut out as me . . . God, I'm scared, Shakey. Tell me what to do.

He felt the gun jabbing hard against his skin. It seemed like a huge bulge, so he bent forward, hunching his tall frame and sucking in his stomach. Fragments of thoughts—tall stacks of money, bills stamped PAID in bold black letters—whirled in his head. His boots stomped the cement dully. No trash on this sidewalk, the wind had scoured it clear. No winos in these gutters, no room for them in this town. Skip the wine. The habit he couldn't break was food. He was in a survival rut.

The dark gray shape of a small deli appeared like a wish. He could steal his loaf of bread there. He could go in and order up a whole sack of eats and tell them to stuff the tab and then run like hell. Sure, run. And where do you hide in Podunk? No, if he was going to try anything, it had to be the Captain Midnight thing. No cars in the drive up, nobody going in or coming out, it was the right kind of place for a first shot. If he was really going to do it. *Am I really going to do it, Shakey*? He trembled.

A mangy-looking tomcat sniffed hungrily along the crack at the base of the deli's door. Its coat was caked and matted and its yellow chest fur clung to its ribs. "Good hunting, old pal," Donald called softly after the tom as it stalked off, twitching its tail in seeming disgust.

If it was ever going to be time, the time had come. *Take a deep breath. Keep a stiff upper lip. Think of the Captain*. He closed his eyes and tried to summon up the old pictures of gold bars and precious gems spilling out of treasure chests, but they wouldn't come to him. Eyes still shut, he reached out unwillingly for the door handle.

The tinkling sound of the tin bell over the door ricocheted off shelves of dusty canned goods and gradually died away in his ears as he stood on the threshold, blinking in the dimness. Pale sunshine had followed him in, throwing the ugly blot of his shadow across the plank floor, splashing against the counter front and across its scarred and pitted top, flaming the skewer of an old-fashioned ticket spindle.

Waiting for his eyes to adjust to the interior dimness, he slowly closed the door behind him, causing the bell to ring again. Someone must hear the bell, he knew, but no one spoke. Over the counter, an old school clock whirred and clicked in the silence. Donald thrust his hands in his pockets, then jerked one back out to scratch the itchy stubble on his chin.

His narrowed eyes darted round the small shop, eager to size up the risks he ran confined within these walls, to find alternate escape routes. If he was going to do something, he'd have to be ready to get away. Be prepared, the Boy Scout motto. Was that another door there at the back? Just an open john, smelling of cheap disinfectant. He nodded. Could come in handy later.

His view cleared slowly, like a Polaroid photo developing. He swaggered toward the display cases, past the cash register. Only then did an old woman clerk—Clara, from her name tag—appear there behind the counter ghostlike with luminous green eyes to ask him if she might help him.

He almost laughed. Help him? Old Clara in your blue flower dress, you don't know it yet, but you're going to be a real big help. Too bad it has to be your shift. Somebody's got to mind the store, but why not somebody else, somebody not so . . . what the hell, what's it to me? She's nothing, nothing but a rag mop in a blue sack.

"Is there something wrong, young man?"

Wrong? You got it, old lady. His hand reached out, his finger tip touched the spindle. He had to pick it up, feel its thin coldness. But stick to business. Tell her. Now, Shakey? Do it.

He spun around to face her. "The money. All of it. Now!" he shouted, feeling like an actor playing a tough guy in a cheap flick. It didn't sound like he meant it, no real edge to his voice, just a dumb loud noise. She stared at him like she hadn't heard. Then he remembered—it's not a stickup till you show your "gat." No wonder she was staring. He fumbled in his shirt, pulled out the cap pistol, and pointed it at her, waving it back and forth to keep her from seeing it wasn't real. Some Captain Midnight, huh Shakey?

Still she stood there motionless, refusing to obey. Had he scared her that bad? Or was she daring him to do something? How could she be scared when it was so ridiculous? But someone could come in any minute. He could hear Captain Midnight: *Not that way, Stupid. Closer!*

He ran round the counter behind her, touched the gun barrel to her ear. "I said now," he growled, chewing the words. He felt her body stiffen beneath the gun, then start to swivel round to face him. He wasn't going to meet those accusing green mama eyes again. "You stay put!" he commanded. Which meant getting the money from the register himself. Not supposed to go like this, Shakey, is it? Captain Midnight doesn't run into penny-ante problems.

"Are you sure you want to do this?" Clara asked.

"Goddam, lady, you shut up, hear me? I don't want to hurt you." He shoved her against the counter, shifted his gun to his left hand and stepped over to the cash register. Jesus, what's a dump like this doing with a computer? What key—Total? Subtotal?

The cash tray shot open with a loud ching-buzz, the old woman jumped, and he felt like he'd hit a jackpot. The payoff was there for the taking, so easy. This was really it, he was actually going to do a robbery—him, Donald Kell, not Captain Midnight. The bins of bills were like ripe fruit: ones, fives, tens. No twenties. OK. He didn't need a fortune. Just enough to get him out of this godforsaken burg.

A stack of brown sacks under the counter became part of his luck, part of the plan. He popped one open and set it down beside the register. The bills felt dusty dirty to his clutching hand as he moved them from till to sack, and he rubbed his palm against his pant leg. His face itched, but he didn't want to touch it with his dirty fingers. *Easy, boy,* whispered the voice from the tales. *Don't lose your cool now.* Donald took a deep breath.

"OK, get in there." He motioned at the open rest room, nudging her that way. He had to keep prodding her forward, all the way to the wall beside the toilet. "Now just stand there quiet. You start yelling, I'll come back here and shut you up."

Slowly he backed out of the foul-smelling room. A pressure on his hip, his shirttail caught on an invisible nail, he hung there a long second, unable to move. A tug, a rip, he tore free. The woman began to turn toward him again, to speak, to accuse.

He slammed the door shut. "You stay right there, facing that wall!" he screamed, trembling. He turned to leave, froze in his tracks, turned back to the door. "I'm sorry," he muttered. "You seem like a nice lady. You just happened to be here, that's all."

Before going back outside, he paused to arrange his thoughts. But his thoughts swirled and would not come together into ideas of any use. He wiped sweat from his forehead with his shirt sleeve, saw that he still had the cap pistol in his hand, and dropped it in the money sack. Idiot! What else was he overlooking? Criminals couldn't afford to be so careless. He folded the sack and hugged it to his chest, pushed the door open with his foot, and went out.

The sun was paler, the wind colder than when he'd gone in. He told himself not to run or look behind him or do anything else that would mark him as suspicious. But he couldn't help how he felt—alone, sick, lost. Living on borrowed time. How much? How long before the old bag would call the cops on him?

He'd said he'd shut her up. Maybe he should have put her

out. But he couldn't have hit her. He couldn't really hurt anyone, not an old woman with those green eyes.

His boot turned, twisting his ankle, and he pitched forward, falling on top of the sack, which he kept clutched tight against his chest. For a few seconds he lay half sprawled on the cold cement, panting to get his breath back. His gut churned, a bitter taste rose in his throat. Better find some place fast, he thought, staggering to his feet. He didn't get far.

Pain carved him with a glass cutter's edge as he grabbed for the corner of the gray stone building. He doubled over, retching violently. Yet in spite of the ripping and tearing in his stomach and his burning throat, nothing had ever felt so good. He spewed his system clean. Over . . . he thought, finally over . . . Standing again, he looked up to a weathered painted sign above his head: CAROL COU TY B S DEPOT.

His sack now pressed more to his stomach than his chest, he plunged inside and headed for the men's toilets. Somebody had scrawled a "Help Wanted" sign above the grimy urinals. With a wry smile he went into a stall and sat down on the stool. He let out a sigh of thanks for the privacy of toilet stalls and began unfolding his puke-flecked sack.

Right on top, his cap gun. Cap'n Cap-gun, that's me. Big shot, pow pow. He pointed the barrel at the ceiling and pulled the trigger, click click click. Oh, he was one fierce dude, scaring old ladies and being so scared by an old lady's eyes he had to throw up on main street. What kind of pantywaist pulled that kind of shenanigan? He wiped the toy with his shirttail. Could it matter if a cap gun had his fingerprints on it? Did fingerprints even stick to cap guns? What difference did it make?

He lifted the lid of the toilet's water tank and dropped the gun into the scummy green water. Somebody'd find it in ten years, next time they cleaned up. "Bye bye, Cap'n," he cooed, setting the lid back.

Now how much bread? Lots of ones, not so many fives and tens. A lousy seventy-eight bucks. Didn't come close to paying for all that sweat. He could always flush the lot down the pipe and just walk out of this stinking town. If *he* didn't have anything on him, then *they* didn't have anything on him either. Except the old woman could finger him. She'd looked him over good enough. Damn! Why hadn't he been smart enough to cover his face. Because he was dumb. He slammed his fist into the metal door of the stall and felt it shake on weak hinges. Everything in this place is falling apart, and it's taking me down with it.

A fresh surge of nausea hit his gut and he felt his bowels contract. He flung up the toilet seat, yanked at his belt buckle. His body was getting rid of everything he'd stuffed into it the past two days, dumping the muck, trying to make a clean start. He felt the strain ease, muscles loosen. His shoulders hunched forward, his forehead rested on his palms.

When he reached out for the roller, he found it empty and broken. A job for somebody . . . But what in hell was he expected to do in the meantime? The brown money sack lay at his feet. Tear away the top part of it. God, what a lousy way to spend a day.

He stood up, pressed the flush handle. Water roared into the toilet bowl and kept running. He jiggled the handle, but the water wouldn't stop. Big deal. Who cares? It could run forever and not get anywhere. Like someone he knew.

He remembered the cap gun. That's what was keeping the water going. If he fished it out, the water'd probably stop. But why bother? It wasn't his problem any more. He was leaving. Yeah, by god, he was. He was clearing out. He actually believed it. Yeah.

A bold splash of color, a collage of graffiti above the tank, caught his eye. "Call Mary for a good . . ." "If yer so smart, whatcha doin here?" "How many bankers does it take to screw a farmer?" One in particular stood out from the rest. Some would-be caricature artist had drawn President Reagan in a monk's cowl, wildly waving a sign that read: JUNKIE GO HOME! First he spat at it. Then he flipped it off. Then he laughed. Sure, why not? Takes all kinds of junkies to make a great country like ours. Hey, maybe I'll just do that, Mr. President.

Tucking his money into his shirt, he walked out of the rest room and headed for the bus ticket counter.

INDEX

H

I

J

K

L

M

O

P

R

S

T

U

W